André Gorz
A Critical Introduction

Conrad Lodziak
and Jeremy Tatman

Pluto Press

LONDON · CHICAGO, IL.

First published 1997 by Pluto Press
345 Archway Road, London N6 5AA
and 1436 West Randolph,
Chicago, Illinois 60607, USA

British Library Cataloguing in Publication Data
A catalogue record for this book is available from the British Library

ISBN 0 7453 0786 8 hbk

Library of Congress Cataloging in Publication Data
Tatman, Jeremy.
    André Gorz: a critical introduction/Jeremy Tatman and Conrad
Lodziak.
        p.   cm. — (Modern European thinkers)
    Includes bibliographical references and index.
    ISBN 0–7453–0786–8 (hc)
    1. Gorz, André. 2. Social scientists—Biography. 3. Social
sciences—Philosophy. I. Lodziak, Conrad. II. Title.
III. Series.
H59.G67T37   1997
320.53'15'092—dc21
    [B]   96–51821
                                                          CIP

Designed and produced for Pluto Press by
Chase Production Services, Chadlington, OX7 3LN
Typeset from disk by Stanford DTP Services, Milton Keynes
Printed in Great Britain

Contents

For Peg Lodziak and Jo and John Tatman

Acknowledgements

Special thanks are due to: André Gorz for his inspirational writings and for agreeing to be interviewed; Finn Bowring for his expert guidance; and Anne Beech of Pluto Press for her thorough criticisms of the first draft of this book. Thanks are also due to Luke Goode, Josephine Logan, Gabriel Mythen, Jim Shorthose and Josué Pereira da Silva.

Introduction

In 1978 Herbert Gintis referred to André Gorz as 'the greatest of modern French social thinkers', who 'dares to venture where no one really has before', and who 'has taken up where Herbert Marcuse left off'.[1] This estimation of the value of Gorz's work does have its supporters but, not surprisingly, given the controversial nature of much of Gorz's writings, it is not a view that is universally shared. We are not sufficiently familiar with modern French social thought to confidently make the kind of judgement advanced by Gintis. We do, however, agree with Gintis that Gorz, though obviously not a member of the Frankfurt School of critical social theory, is the best contemporary exponent of that tradition.

That someone as highly respected as Gintis showers praise on Gorz's thought is reason enough to embark upon a text introducing Gorz's work. Gorz's writings do crop up in a number of places – in the study of modern European thought, of existential Marxism, of politics, of ecology, of post-industrialism, of the social impact of technology, of labour process, in the critique of capitalism, in debates on guaranteed income, and so on. We want to maintain that the value of Gorz's contributions to these fields of study and debate can be best understood against the backdrop of an appreciation of the *whole* of his work. This alone provides a second reason for this volume.

A third reason, one often invoked in projects of this kind, does not apply here. A common justification for an introductory text on a major thinker is that which emphasises 'the difficulty' and 'inaccessibility' of the thinker's writings. Such a justification can readily translate into 'the need to interpret' the thinker's work. Of course interpretation is vulnerable to error and misrepresentation, and thus to misleading the reader. Luckily for us these dangers are minimised by the very accessibility of Gorz's writings. Gorz may well require the reader to think, and to think hard, but he does make his meaning explicitly clear. Even so, Gorz has been misrepresented. Correcting these misrepresentations does suggest another good reason for an introductory text on Gorz.

Misrepresentation can take many forms and have several sources. A common misrepresentation of Gorz arises from a standard technique adopted in academic writing. Many academics are in the habit of embellishing sentences with a referenced 'throwaway' phrase. The intended purpose of this technique is to impress the reader with the author's breadth of knowledge. In some cases this technique produces the opposite effect – it reflects the author's ignorance, that is, it tells us something about the author's lack of knowledge, that he or she has not actually read the referenced text. Thus in various places we encounter a sentence which begins: 'In spite of what Gorz thinks, the working classes have not disappeared ...'. The reference is of course to Gorz's most famous book, *Farewell to the Working Class*. Needless to say, reading the title of a book can never be a substitute for reading the book itself. In many respects the inappropriate citing of *Farewell to the Working Class* parallels what has happened to Marcuse's *One-Dimensional Man*. This book is often cited as an overly pessimistic treatment of the extent to which individuals have lost their capacity for autonomy. Yet an actual reading of the book, rather than the title only, reveals that this is far from the case.[2]

These kinds of misrepresentations are unfortunate in so far as they may discourage students from reading authors such as Gorz and Marcuse. The writings of both of these theorists do constitute a vital resource for those seeking the development of a social order beyond capitalism in which the freedom of everyone can be meaningfully expanded. This, we maintain, is the most important of all reasons for this particular introductory text. Our primary task is to encourage the reader to engage directly with Gorz's writings.

In saying this we recognise that we are going against the grain. All sorts of fashions and changes are afoot in universities which work against the reading of major theorists, and which also increase the likelihood of misrepresentation. While the problem of misrepresentation has always been present, in recent times a particular academic fashion, poststructuralism, has encouraged an approach to the interpretation of texts that ignores the important distinction between theoretical and non-theoretical texts. In poststructuralism the text itself is given priority as a 'reality' irrespective of any reality beyond itself to which it may refer. Any concern with representation is thus removed, and as a consequence, the potential for misrepresentation is increased considerably. Such a move is justified, so it is argued, because a text is first and foremost a product of its own use of language. More precisely, in the words of Tony Bennett, the text is the product of 'the relationship between signs, the play of signification upon signification within a structured field of ideological relationships'.[3] Bennett also tells us that 'the validity of positing a duality between the plane of signification and that of "reality" has long since been called into question in linguistics and literary and film criticism'.[4]

Quite clearly under the influence of poststructuralism innovative interpretations of fictional texts are promoted. But to suppose that this approach has any validity for the interpretation of theoretical texts is to violate the primary purpose of theory. Jürgen Habermas in criticising Jacques Derrida, a major influence on the poststructuralist fashion, acknowledges 'that even the language of the sciences is shot through with metaphors', and he states that 'this is plainly true of the language of philosophy'. But, he argues,

> one cannot, like Derrida, conclude from the unavoidably rhetorical character of *every* kind of language, including philosophical language, that it is all one and the same – that the categories of everyday life and literature, science and fiction, poetry and philosophy, collapse into each other. For Derrida all cats are grey in the night of 'writing'.[5]

Additionally, poststructuralism, in emphasising the meaning generating character of texts, treats the text as having autonomy – an autonomy cut off from authorial intent. Texts can be interpreted without any reference to their authors. Again, we can see the value of this for fictional texts. Indeed a writer of fiction may often deliberately disguise his or her intent, purposefully thwarting interpretations based on authorial intent. But this will not do for theoretical texts. The explicit expression of intent is a defining characteristic of theoretical work.

Poststructuralism is influential in media and cultural studies, and thus to some extent in social theory. While most social and political theorists would agree that poststructuralism has nothing to contribute to the interpretation of theoretical texts, its influence can be seen in the recent proliferation of cavalier interpretations of theory. Gorz, in spite of the clarity of his writing, has, as we shall see later, been carelessly misinterpreted. Poststructuralism may well be a joke, but it does provide a pseudo-justification for poor scholarship – and it forms part of an intellectual climate which dovetails conveniently with recent changes in the universities and in the society–university relation.

The contradictions inherent in the advanced capitalist societies are shaking up traditional socialisation practices. While the consequences of this are by no means uniform, let alone unidirectional, it is provoking many young people into a radical questioning of their place and future in society. Critical social theory in general, and Gorz's writings in particular, address many of the concerns expressed by young people today. In many respects critical social theory has become more relevant as more individuals experience their superfluousness as individuals in the capitalist system. But whereas in the past teachers and academics managed to preserve some spaces in which a radical self-questioning could flourish, such spaces are currently under threat.

The main threat to these spaces comes from economic forces. As capitalist states continuously seek ways of cutting public expenditure, public provision for education has declined. The costs of education, particularly university education, are increasingly borne by the 'consumer', that is by the student. The declining value of student grants in conjunction with the rising costs of being a student, particularly accommodation costs, means that more students than ever before are having to take up casual employment in order to survive. As a consequence less time is available for study, that is for reading and thinking. This alone is bad news for those areas of study, such as critical social theory, that are heavily dependent on the student having time to think. But matters have been made worse by the response of universities to underfunding. In the absence of collective resistance to government cuts, universities are left to compete with each other for dwindling funds. To render themselves 'more competitive', universities have restructured their courses, massaged their images, and have marketed themselves with all the hype typically associated with crude advertising. The restructuring of courses has been conducted in terms of what managers (lightweight and failed academics) of the enterprise (the university) think is likely to attract customers (students). Emphasis is placed on supermarket-style 'variety' and 'choice'. Courses have become heavily fragmented. As a consequence, student workloads have almost doubled. With almost twice as much work to do and less time to do it in, thinking has been marginalised. Understandably students seek 'shortcuts' in their studies. This is especially the case for students on multidisciplinary courses. These courses tend to generate a vast range of unrelated demands which spread students' attention even more thinly than on specialised courses.

Needless to say, the university context of today is increasingly unfriendly to the suggestion that students should engage directly with the writings of important theorists. However useful Gorz might be, undergraduates are less likely to find out.

The commodification of higher education which threatens to obliterate thinking has its complement in publishing. Academic publishers, who are in the business of selling books, know only too well that sales are more likely to be achieved if books are tailored to popular courses. Introductory texts paraphrasing the ideas of original thinkers serve courses made up of a series of introductory summaries of the same ideas. The restructuring of courses, in Britain at least, has come about at a time when 'research output' has gained in importance in the competition for funds. The pressure to publish, especially in the new universities, has grown beyond all recognition. But, especially in the new universities, this pressure is exerted at a time when workloads for academics have been increased considerably. So, on the one hand, changes in higher education have generated the need among students for introductory texts, and texts that might serve as a time-saving substitute for the real thing, and, on the other, these changes have created insecure academics who are prepared to supply this need. What we have is the academic and the student unhappily colluding in commodified surperficiality.

As higher education is increasingly subordinated to the dictates of economic rationality, both in terms of serving the needs of a free-market economy, and in terms of selling its services to the student-consumer, there is a danger that the non-commodifiable will be inappropriately commodified or, and this amounts to the same thing, will cease to exist altogether. This would seem to be the trend at the undergraduate level at least. Obviously we want to work against this trend. This means that we break with the format most commonly adopted in books of this kind – the paraphrase. The paraphrase format is the main means through which thought is inappropriately commodified. Not only does such a format make for superficiality and over-simplification, but the unavoidable reductions involved in paraphrasing can also produce misrepresentations. This is particularly true in the case of attempts to paraphrase critical social theory. In referring to Theodor Adorno, Martin Jay tells us that 'true philosophy, he [Adorno] was fond of insisting, is the type of thinking that resists paraphrase'.[6]

In introducing Gorz some paraphrasing of his writings will be inevitable. But this is not the same thing as using the paraphrase as a *format*. Adorno's essential point is that critical social theory ('true philosophy') cannot be reduced to an identifiable set of ideas however much the commodifiers of knowledge attempt to do this. The publishing and teaching practices involved in the attempted commodification of critical thought transform ideas into dead pseudo-knowledge by failing, in their reductiveness, to pose the full existentiality of the problems addressed by critical theorists. What characterises critical social theory is not so much the ideas that it throws up but the thought processes that it promotes. The insights generated by critical social theory cannot be learned by rote, they can *only* be arrived at by thinking along with the theorist. Gorz, more so than most critical social theorists, enables us to do this.

Instead of a paraphrase format we shall adopt a format which enables us to introduce Gorz in a way which reflects our own thinking along with Gorz, and which hopefully encourages the reader to read Gorz. What we are about to embark upon should in no way be read as a convenient shortcut or substitute for reading Gorz. Of course our thinking along with Gorz does not guarantee a perfect reading or interpretation of Gorz. One has only to consider the wide range of interpretations of Marx's work – all written by those claiming to think along with Marx – to appreciate that we are not invoking a foolproof methodological principle. But we can state what our own method of thinking along with Gorz entails.

First we assume that theoretical work is a self-consciously rational enterprise in which the theorist's intentions are made explicit. Being a rational undertaking it can be supposed that theory will be developed in a manner consistent with the theorist's intent. It is just this which is the basis of the theory's self-consistency. In order to think along with Gorz, or any other major theorist, requires that we first identify what it is that gives a theorist's total project internal consistency.

Second, to think along with Gorz involves understanding a particular text, or part of a text, as a part of Gorz's total project. Bob Jessop spells this out when he states that

> it is worth stating a general methodological rule for the study of Marxist political theory. Namely, when a theorist presents a whole series of concepts and principles of explanation concerned with a particular problem, they must be considered as a connected and reciprocally qualifying system rather than treated in isolation or in a unilateral fashion.[7]

The application of the two general rules outlined above, we believe, ensures, as far as is possible, an understanding of theory coincidental with the author's understanding of it. Further, we insist that these rules be enacted *prior to* subjecting the theoretical text to criticism. Failure to do this has spawned an academic industry of premature, misdirected and thus inappropriate criticism. Most helpful in avoiding these problems is a close reading of the various interviews Gorz has given. Interviews tend to contain Gorz's most explicitly self-conscious statements about his project, and clarify common misunderstandings of his work.

Gorz's project

Underpinning the whole of Gorz's work is an unshakeable commitment to freedom. It is a developing commitment – away from abstract freedom expressed in his early philosophical writings, and towards a concrete, experiential freedom. Since it is only individuals who experience, it is a commitment to the freedom of the individual. Furthermore Gorz's commitment develops into a commitment to the freedom of all individuals. It is thus a commitment to freedom and equality and justice. And this is what sets it apart from all those ideologies of individual freedom that promote and mask social inequalities and injustices.

In the not too distant past any concern for individual freedom tended to be received by some Marxists as a manifestation of 'bourgeois ideology', and in particular the ideology of individualism. Existentialism as a philosophy of individual freedom was thus seen as bourgeois ideology, and humanistic Marxism, socialist humanism and existential Marxism, which all embrace a concern for individual freedom, were derided as forms of 'bourgeois revisionism'. To the dogmatic Marxists, for whom bourgeois revisionism is the worst of all sins, Gorz is a sinner. Luckily this breed of dogmatic Marxists is dying out.

It is Gorz's commitment to individual freedom that enables him radically to criticise both the politics and social policies of dogmatic Marxism, and the oppressive character of capitalist society. Of the former Gorz asks: 'How can we talk about "social emancipation", if what we mean by this is a collective process which takes place over the heads of real individuals?'[8] He continues:

> Liberation as a collective process which we do not all experience as our own individual liberation is precisely the 'educational dictatorship' so far practised by the Church, the omniscient Leninist party and the armed avant-garde. If in fighting for collective liberation we use methods which continue to make individuals the willing tools of something transcendental, then the means intended to bring about liberation will, in fact, continue to devour it.[9]

For Gorz 'collective liberation must always be individual liberation as well'. He emphasises that 'it is important that the starting point for the struggle for collective liberation is in the individual's own desire for liberation'.[10] But he also emphasises that individual freedom in hostile social conditions can only be developed through collective action.

> The question of social emancipation only arises because the real subjects, the individuals, feel social circumstances to be irreconcilable with the development of their own freedom. The social negation of each individual's experience of freedom is the experience of alienation common to us all and this can only be overcome through common action, as we change society.[11]

The 'social negation of each individual's experience of freedom' is something that Gorz is particularly sensitive to. It is for Gorz the basis of his wide-ranging critique of a society subordinated to capitalism. He is arguably at his sharpest in identifying how the supposed freedoms we have, whether in the workplace or in the shopping mall, are pseudo-freedoms which negate our autonomy. He notes how with 'the collapse of "real socialism"' in Central and Eastern Europe, people thought that 'they would enter the realm

of freedom, prosperity, security and justice'. But, he says, 'They
were wrong.' Instead they have got a right-wing government that

> represents the market, competition, productivist imperatives,
> lust for profit and love of gain; it represents letting the weakest
> go to the wall, dismantling social security and the public services,
> unemployment for a third – and soon, perhaps, for half – of the
> workforce of the former GDR, among others. They have,
> admittedly, been delivered from the totalitarian order, which
> is all well and good, and now they have freedom – but 'freedom
> to do what?'.[12]

To think along with Gorz involves empathising with the experience
of the most oppressed. Experience is the primary data of thought
and theory. But while the individual's reflections on his or her own
experience can make for a valid psychology, it is an insufficient basis
for understanding society. Society cannot speak for itself. It does,
of course, attempt to do this through the self-appointed privileged
or through their elected political representatives. But since one of
the primary purposes of these voices of representation is to conceal
the very power they represent, we get a depiction of society that
is to say the least, misleading. In fact what we get is a
(mis)understanding of society, which is to say that we get the
dominant ideology. In order to understand society it is thus
necessary to distance ourselves from the voices of the most powerful.
As Jean-Paul Sartre put it, 'The only way the intellectual can really
distance himself from the official ideology decreed from above is
by placing himself alongside those whose very existence contradicts
it.'[13] And since the practices of the most powerful create the
oppressed, and impact most fully and intensely on them, it follows
that a more complete understanding of what makes a society what
it is is more likely to be achieved from the existential location of
the oppressed than from anywhere else. Gorz has the uncanny ability
to stand alongside the most oppressed. His social theory is
understanding and critique rolled into one.

There is little point in social theory and critique unless it serves
social emancipation. Marx's eleventh thesis on Feuerbach – 'The
philosophers have only *interpreted* the world, in various ways; the
point, however, is to *change* it' – is lost on those academics who
approach social theory and critique as little more than a fund of
'interesting ideas' to be studied and debated. Marx's thesis, however,
is certainly not lost on Gorz. The whole of Gorz's work is dedicated
to emancipatory social change. At a stretch this might be said of
other critical social theorists. But Gorz, more than any other critical
social theorist, does not let matters rest with radical critique. He
is forever spelling out the practical implications of his thinking. To
think along with Gorz is to think practically, both in the here and

now, and into a future beyond capitalism. Furthermore, it is a thinking that is pregnant with a sense of urgency. It is as if Gorz is saying: 'Here are the possibilities for greater freedom. We can make this happen together. Let's do it *now*.'

Given our emphasis on thinking along with Gorz, it would seem to make sense to organise our engagement with Gorz in a way that reflects the chronology of his thinking. While, as we have already indicated, there are underlying currents common to the whole of Gorz's thinking, there are also shifts in emphasis and orientation. It would be most surprising if no changes occurred throughout 50 years of writing. Further, as a social theorist reflecting on society, one might expect Gorz to respond to significant social changes. There appears to be a period around the mid-1970s when Gorz's thinking took off in new directions. First, in reflecting on the events of May 1968 in Paris, and cultural movements and revolts elsewhere, Gorz not only realised that traditional left politics held little appeal to younger generations, but also that cultural shifts suggested that emancipatory politics had to be radically reformulated. Part of his new thinking embodied many of the concerns and style of the new social movements, and was expressed in his development of political ecology. Second, Gorz saw in the micro-electronic revolution new possibilities for freedom. Freedom from work rather than freedom within work emerged as a dominant theme in Gorz's writings. And it is a theme central to his conception of political ecology.

We can thus make a loose distinction between the earlier and the later Gorz. This is reflected in the division between the second and third chapters. The fourth chapter discusses criticisms that have been levelled at Gorz, and we conclude with a recent interview with Gorz. First, however, we present a biographical sketch of Gorz.

1

Victim and Accomplice

> Can you, starting from nothing, that is from yourself, recreate
> everything, restore everything? When the accidents of birth and
> history mean that you belong to no people or group, that no
> culture, ideology, class or value system strike you immediately
> as being yours, can you – and if so, according to what criteria
> – choose to prefer any one class, value, action or behaviour to
> all others?[1]

In the Preface to the belatedly published *Fondements pour une
morale* André Gorz reveals that prior to embarking upon this
philosophical treatise in 1945, the above questions had preoccupied
his thoughts and ultimately stimulated his interest in existentialist
philosophy. The questions themselves directly correspond to Gorz's
own experience of social isolation and estrangement during this
period. His desire to resolve them, described by Gorz as 'indistin-
guishable from the very endeavour of living',[2] reflected his longing
to transcend the perennial feelings of alienation and illegitimacy
to which they allude.

Gorz's earliest writings, including *Fondements pour une morale* and
the later, autobiographical, *Le Traître*,[3] may be considered as
testimonies to this desire. On the one hand, from a theoretical
perspective, these texts are of importance for their development of
the central Gorzian themes of freedom and alienation. As a number
of theorists have demonstrated, in this respect they provide the
philosophical foundations for much of Gorz's more contemporary
and celebrated works.[4] Beyond this, however, these books have a
further significance in that they represent the method and the
process of their author's prolonged existential journey from acute
personal crisis towards self-affirmation.

Still unavailable in English, *Fondements pour une morale* was
originally conceived of as a three-volume continuation of Jean-Paul
Sartre's *Being and Nothingness*.[5] The first volume, finally published
in 1977, was an attempt to explore further fundamental questions
which Sartre had raised, without fully addressing, in his seminal
text. In particular, Gorz was concerned 'to broach the questions
of morality, authenticity and the forms of self-analysis necessary
for the "existential conversion"'[6] implied by Sartre. However, like

a number of other theorists of that time, Gorz was not entirely convinced by Sartre's existential ethics. As Finn Bowring points out:

> *Being and Nothingness* failed to convincingly demonstrate how one could achieve the elusive condition of authenticity, how one could judge, value and choose from any superior standpoint, and how, through the 'radical conversion' intimated by Sartre, one could reconcile oneself with the fundamental ambiguities of the human condition.[7]

It is precisely these issues, on both a personal and a philosophical level, which continued to perplex Gorz, defining the parameters of his enquiry.[8] As the solution to these questions could not be derived from Sartre's ontology itself, Gorz attempted to refound the Sartrian method, 'rebuilding it in such a way that the "cogito" progressively provided the tools for *thinking* that which it grasped prior to any discourse'.[9] Towards this end he endeavoured to transcend the schematic rigidity for which Sartre had been criticised,[10] inflecting his ontological foundation and emphasising the three-dimensional nature of the conscious being.[11] In particular, as Gorz was later to explain, he sought to demonstrate 'that we always exist on several different planes with their corresponding differently structured relations to being and value'.[12]

By the time that Gorz had completed the first volume of *Fondements pour une morale*, some eight years later in 1955, he had moved to France from Switzerland and had established a close personal friendship with Sartre. Indeed it was to Sartre's Parisian apartment that Gorz, with considerable trepidation, initially took his completed manuscript. However, following years of impassioned debate with French Marxists, Sartre's own position had changed considerably from that presented in *Being and Nothingness*.[13] Engaged upon his own major venture to wed existential phenomenology with historical materialism,[14] Sartre now considered ontology and moral philosophy to be 'outmoded errors'. Subsequently, when Gorz returned to reclaim his work some six weeks later, there had been practically no discussion of its content. In fact it was unclear if his friend had even got beyond the first page: 'Had Sartre read much more of it? It was probably best not to enquire: that would not achieve anything.'[15] On that same day Gorz had received a word of recommendation from Jean Hyppolite, 'from whom, added Sartre, one should not expect too much: nobody had the power to make a publisher accept this immoderate work by an unknown author'.[16] They never talked of the matter again.

If Gorz's response to this setback was understandably one of disappointment, he was not entirely surprised. Revealing his persistent sense of illegitimacy at the time, he recalls:

Thus, everything turned out as he had always expected it would. During the eight or nine years that he was working on the *thing* he kept telling himself that nobody would ever read it, that they would laugh in his face and seek to punish him for what they took to be his presumption. He lived in the anticipation of this setback. He never thought that he could succeed in any way whatever: there was nothing about him that could suit or please other people ... This is why he did not even struggle. What happened was quite *normal*.[17]

Having anticipated such an unfavourable response to his first manuscript, Gorz had already taken precautionary measures prior to its submission to Sartre. Essentially abandoning the final two, unrevised volumes of *Fondements pour une morale*, Gorz began to devote himself to writing the autobiographical essay *The Traitor*. The 'application and test bench' of its predecessor's method of self-conversion to Gorz's own life, this quickly became of greater significance to him than anything else. Indeed, the submission of this second manuscript, nine months later, 'was, in fact, his renunciation of the publication of the first'.[18]

Combining autobiography with philosophical enquiry and confession, *The Traitor* remains one of the most intimate and profound books to have emerged from the existentialist movement.[19] In terms of its aims, method and style it is a work which pushes uncomfortably against the boundaries of the autobiographical genre,[20] defying both formalised synopsis or summary classification.[21] Most accurately defined as 'a mercurial, abstruse and obsessively intellectual self-portrait' it is a text which self-consciously 'demonstrates the tortuously reflective character of the person it portrays',

> ceaselessly turning back on itself, qualifying its conclusions, analysing its observations, perpetually revising its appraisal of the very same process of self-reconstruction, taking each new insight as further material to interrogate and display, to uncover as vital authentication of the author's testimony.[22]

Drawing extensively upon Marxist, psychoanalytic and existentialist theories, *The Traitor* represents Gorz's meticulous examination of the history of his relationship to his own body, to his environment and to society in general. Central to his painstaking endeavour, which is uniquely illuminated by the honest recall of personal experience, is Gorz's attempt to comprehend, and ultimately liberate himself from, his state of 'absolute subjective misery'. Within this process, as befitting the time and the mood in which it was written, Gorz exposes what he considers to be the limitations of the Western philosophical heritage in accounting for both the person that he has and could become. It is precisely this intensive and innovative deployment of theory, as a means of comprehending himself and his situation, which for many remains the primary interest in the text.[23] However, as a text in which Gorz seeks to comprehend the complexity of his past, as well as his possibilities within the present and the future, *The Traitor* also offers the reader a 'profound and poignant insight into the lived experience of its alienated protagonist'.[24] In this respect, as Bowring has demonstrated, it is a work which provides a valuable means of comprehending the early development of Gorz's thinking, by allowing us to explore the relationship between his life and his work as it has been lived and understood by the author himself.

Our use of *The Traitor* in this chapter will reflect the need to provide a bare minimum of autobiographical facts and Gorz's recall of significant experiences in his childhood, youth and early adulthood. However, the chapter will focus primarily upon the character and the consequences of Gorz's retrospective self-analysis. These are, after all, particularly useful in providing insights into Gorz's early and subsequent motivations and thinking. The reader should bear in mind that for the majority of this text, in a manner reflecting his continuing sense of self-alienation, Gorz refers to himself in the third person.

Childhood and adolescence

At the time of writing *The Traitor* Gorz was, by his own admission, 'nothing but a tangle of objective contradictions which came to him from the outside and of which he was not clearly aware'.[25] However, it seems that this absence of any tangible sense of self could, at least partially, be explicated precisely in terms of the transitory and conflicting identities which had been conferred upon him at different stages of his young life. Born in Vienna in 1924, Gorz was the only son of an unhappy marriage between his Christian mother and Jewish father. From an early age, undoubtedly influenced by the racial intolerance he experienced both within and beyond the parameters of his own family, Gorz, like many of those around him, attributed considerable significance to his ambiguous cultural identity. This was to remain a source of considerable personal anxiety for many years to come.

Within a context of rising anti-semitism in Austria during the 1920s and 1930s, Gorz's childhood and early adolescence was primarily characterised by feelings of worthlessness and despair. On the one hand, on account of his Jewish lineage, he felt increasingly repudiated by sections of the indigenous population, while, on the other hand, within the besieged Semitic community, he feared he was not Jewish enough for his opposition to the Reich to be trusted. By the time Austria had been annexed by Germany, parental fears that he would be conscripted had developed to the extent that, at great financial sacrifice, it was decided to send him to a private boarding school abroad. Such were the 'accidents of birth and history' through which Gorz found himself in political exile, dispossessed of his family and his motherland, at the age of fifteen.

Against the imminent backdrop of Germany's invasion of Poland and the Nazi–Soviet pact, Gorz's arrival in Switzerland in 1939 was experienced 'as if he had landed on another planet'.[26] However, while Switzerland provided him with a temporary respite from danger, and a marked contrast to the social and political turmoil that he had left behind, this culturally unfamiliar landscape was to represent a further context in which Gorz would experience marginalisation and distrust.

At the Institut Montana boarding school Gorz quickly experienced a feeling of persecution once more. On the one hand its director, whose Swiss patriotism his mother had appealed to in securing reduced tuition fees, was 'a Nazi drunkard who would take revenge for her success over him'.[27] While among the 60 affluent Dutch, German and Swiss students residing there, Gorz's accent and ignorance of the 'snob' values which formed the basis of their cliques once again transformed him into an 'outsider' and an enduring object of ridicule. Essentially confined to his room of six square yards outside of school hours, Gorz's feelings of isolation quickly intensified in his new environment. Even beyond the boundaries of the school solace was unlikely among a population likely to mistrust him as a German passport holder. In short, there appeared to be no way out of the hostile environment in which he was incarcerated. It seemed to Gorz that 'outside his cell his prison was the whole world'.[28]

Rejected at every turn, Gorz felt the nothingness that he was for others embrace and swell within him. Adopting the criticisms which were directed against him as his own, he concluded that he was wrong to be a Jew; just as he was wrong not to share his peers enthusiasm for jazz, cigarettes and alcohol. With 'pathetic good will' he dedicated himself to understanding the infatuations of those with whom he studied and lived; only for his ingenuous questions to serve as a further pretext and justification for his continued exclusion. It seemed that, regardless of the context, he was powerless to gain the recognition and acceptance of those with whom he came into contact. 'That was when he began feeling that life was unliveable; that man is a wound in which the world turns like a knife; and that between man and the world there was one term too many.'[29]

The intense feelings of illegitimacy and despair articulated here would persist, giving rise to intermittent thoughts of suicide, until

Gorz completed his studies at the University of Lausanne in 1945. Even then with little option but to remain in Switzerland, 'a tedious country' where he clearly did not fit in, it seemed that Gorz's sense of alienation would persist for a number of years to come. Deprived of any sense of cultural belonging, or any conception of what he might feasibly do with his life, the fundamental problem of how he could possibly go on living remained. Neither Jewish, nor Aryan, nor Austrian, nor German, nor Swiss, Gorz had no identity whatsoever upon which he could rely; no path that he was expected to follow. Indeed, his situation was only exacerbated by the plethora of contradictory identities which had been bestowed upon him externally, invariably with negative connotations. Thus, as the Second World War drew to a close, we find that Gorz could only define himself in negative, rather than affirmative terms. He was 'a stateless refugee, a man with no family, no past, no future, no reason for being "here" (insofar as no place deserved to be called here) rather than anywhere else, no reason for doing one thing rather than another'.[30] 'He was ... nothing, in short, except the nothing that he was.'[31]

Early adulthood

A 'stranger to all nations and cultures', Gorz's condition of nullity was characterised by an absence of the cultural commonplaces that those around him took for granted. As a consequence of his feelings of repeated social exclusion, all attitudes and forms of action and existence were experienced as being equally exterior and illegitimate. He was 'a foreign witness to an infinity of possible possibilities, none of which were his'.[32] Caught up in the radical questioning of everything around him, Gorz was incapable of finding or committing himself to any activity through which he could make himself recognisable – either to himself or others. Ultimately, 'he found himself, all in all, in what might be termed a philosophical condition, by virtue of the fundamental nature of the problems he was confronting'.[33] In *The Traitor*, first published in 1956, Gorz clearly articulates the predicament in which he found himself at that time:

> Because I belong nowhere, ... because I am exiled from all groups and enterprises, there is only one alternative: either to be marginal in regard to society and history, the supernumerary of the human race, the pure consumer of air, water, bread, and other people's work, reduced to the boredom of living, to the acute awareness of the contingency of everything around me, or to raise myself in conscience to the absolute – that is, to establish everything philosophically ... and ... to recover, starting from this speculative interest, the taste for the concrete.[34]

With no certainty save that certainties can be acquired and remain subject to dismissal, the twenty-year-old Gorz was at once condemned to create his own certainties and deprived of the cultural basis for this creation. For the want of any substantive cultural foundations, he would have to 'justify everything that he propounded in order to be able to propound anything at all'.[35] His condition of nullity could only be transcended philosophically: he could 'achieve the concrete only by starting from the abstract, the real starting from the Idea'.[36] In the belief that he could only begin living on the day that he had successfully resolved the question of 'when, how [and] for whom can life have a meaning?',[37] it was a project to which Gorz would essentially devote the next eleven years of his life.

His initial problem was where to begin this 'labour of restoration', assuming that it was possible at all. Without the benefit of a formal education in philosophy, he had to establish whether it was possible for individuals to place their social and cultural moulds into brackets and to recover the original meanings and movement of their corporeal life. To begin with, the crucial question was therefore to find a way of ordering the possibilities open to him. He had to establish a criteria through which he could list, group and hierarchise the fundamental human possibilities and values. He reasoned that if no such hierarchy existed, and individuals acted by virtue of their social conditioning alone, 'nothing was any worth: men were, in essence, the product of a condition which was not the conscious product of anyone'.[38] If, on the other hand, Gorz could demonstrate an absolute hierarchy of human possibilities, he would also be able to establish the material circumstances which favoured their ultimate fulfilment. This, essentially, was the task he set himself in *Fondements pour une morale*:

> In short, he had to *found* – in the very precise sense which phenomenology gives to this term – an 'axiology', that is a hierarchy of 'levels' along which existence may develop and a hierarchy of the values which it may pursue there; he had to found a theory of alienation and a moral philosophy.[39]

Jean-Paul Sartre's *Being and Nothingness*, 'the phenomenological ontology conscious of its principles and its basis ... immediately filled the gap for him'.[40] While most philosophical discourses were inevitably a form of communion from which Gorz was to some extent excluded, in Sartre he discovered a philosophy into which he could launch himself without being familiar or erudite with the classics. Starting from nothing and practising the most radical *cogito* possible, Sartre's questioning 'threw every received cultural and intellectual conviction into doubt', before arriving 'at the sole irreducible fact: that consciousness is a being whose being is permanently in question'.[41] He quickly gained the impression that 'Sartrian philosophy moved in the universe of the axioms which remain after all the accumulated experience and "sense sediments" had been swept away'.[42] It was an approach which clearly appealed to Gorz's own heightened sense of contingency and, presenting itself to him as a kind of new beginning, its impact was considerable:

> I steeped myself in *Being and Nothingness*, at first without understanding much of it, fascinated by the novelty and complexity of its thought, then, by dint of persevering in my reading of this great object, infecting myself with it, adopting its terminology, raising it to the dignity of an encyclopaedia which, since it treated everything, must have an answer to everything, and at last living in a universe having *Being and Nothingness* for my frontiers.[43]

Sartrian philosophy ultimately provided Gorz with a means of interpreting himself and the world, instilling within him the enduring belief that a human being was capable of self-emancipation and determination. However, some ten years later, as he approached the completion of *Fondements pour une morale*, Gorz realised that he was essentially the same person as he had been a decade before:

> He had discovered that when a man is incapable of living, or when life has no meaning for him, he always invents this way out for himself: to write about the nonmeaning of life, to look for an explanation, an escape, to demonstrate that all roads are blocked save one – this demonstration itself, and the remedy it provides against the experience it contradicts.[44]

In typically self-critical fashion, Gorz concluded that rather than attempting to resolve his problems in *Fondements pour une morale*, he had tried to get rid of them. While writing the manuscript, he had effectively purged himself of his problems by posing them in the abstract. It was only now that he realised that the essential thing, himself, was still missing. The best that could be said was that he had learned to think more about life, and endure himself less, than he had in the past. In retrospect, however, the project seemed nothing more than 'a sterile evasion'; a means of escaping himself by imitating a technique that was not even his own.[45] '"The Essay" … had given him something to think about for ten years, but these ruminations had not reached him.'[46] Gorz had asked himself the questions that Sartre had left open, but he had refused to *live* them.

The belief that he had made a fundamental and costly error of judgement provoked the following, decisive resolution amidst his anguish:

Everything had to be begun all over again; he must take a look at *himself* rather than at 'man in general'. He must stop thinking that a problem can ever be 'solved'. He must reach this certainty: *A philosophy cannot dispense with life – the question persists and you have to put up with yourself indefinitely.*[47]

With these thoughts in the forefront of his mind, Gorz finally began the process of 'dissecting himself by words' so that he might someday 'create himself by actions'.[48]

Retrospective self-analysis

Sources of self-alienation

In seeking to identify and comprehend the development of his infantile complexes, Gorz begins his analysis prior to his own conception. Recognising the demands and expectations that are placed upon the child prior to it's birth, he acknowledges that:

> Long before our birth, even before we are conceived, parents have decided who we will be. They have called us 'he' before we could say 'I'. We existed at first as absolute objects. By means of our family, society assigns us a situation, a being, a set of roles; the contradictions of history and class struggle determine in advance the character and destiny of generations to come ... Everywhere the role is there, waiting for its man.[49]

The second child of parents divided by religion, race, temperament and values, Gorz's early childhood was dominated by the figure of 'Maria', his socially aspiring mother. Motivated by her ambition to rise above her modest family background, Maria had married 'Jacob' Horst, her nondescript Moravian boss, who was fifteen years her senior.[50] Soon afterwards, in a manner which reflected both her anti-semitic and material values, she persuaded her husband to take over his brother-in-law's crate manufacturing business and renounce both his family and his religion. The birth of André some years later, would be a further means of confirming her belated entry into bourgeois society.

As the final component of her family unit, Maria envisaged Gerhart to be the masculine counterpart to his sister's feminine charm. Named after a German Nobel prize winner whom she admired for his virile good looks, he would be handsome, intelligent and a further index of her own wealth and respectability.[51] However, from the moment of her son's birth, according to Gorz, Maria's maternal passion declined. It deteriorated further when she realised that, in contrast to his namesake, 'her son was ugly, squalling and dark-haired'.[52] This was the first of many occasions when her son would fail to live up to her high expectations.

Gorz's early childhood was marked by the repressive character of bourgeois socialisation and the particular value that his parents attributed to it. To the young Gerhart, the requirements of 'respectable behaviour', as defined by his parents, revealed themselves as a myriad of complex rules and rituals which he neither understood nor seemed capable of satisfying. His persistent failure to meet their opaque standards led him to live in continuous fear of parental condemnation, nurturing the feelings of inadequacy that would accompany him into adulthood. However, the *original* development of these insecurities corresponded to the discovery of his existence for others; for it was here that the fundamental discrepancy between his being-for-himself and his being-for-others initially revealed itself. He recalls:

> This body, which he identified with himself signified something for other people and ... this signification escaped him. The lived meaning of his behaviour was stolen from him by a hedge of faces leaning over him which would suddenly burst out laughing or delivered weighty commentaries having received a mysterious message from his body. This body itself was stolen from him, it spoke to others in a language he did not know.[53]

It was thus that

> Unrealisable significations, intentions he was certain he did not have because he did not understand them, came to inhabit him from outside, establishing themselves within him like parasites that eat away the flesh or, worse still, the consciousness, without him being able to turn around and see them ... They saw something on him he was ignorant of, he 'told' them something he did not know, they expected him to play a role. He did not understand them, he did not understand his role. They terrorised him. He hated them.[54]

Trained and presented as an object of respectability before other adults, Gorz recognised that his existence for others, particularly his mother, was traumatically estranged from his own self-identity. Furthermore, Maria's requirements 'were such that no child could have satisfied them'. On the one hand, she expected him to fulfil the role of the well-brought-up little boy, in order to satisfy her social aspirations; while on the other, although this could only be accomplished by her son through acting, she demanded sincerity. His position, he explains, was entirely untenable:

> Either he was acting and then he was lying, or else he was not lying and then he was disappointing her. He was disappointing her by what he really was, and realizing that he did not come

up to what was expected of him made him lose confidence in his capacity as an actor.[55]

Castigated for both attempted collusion and his spontaneous acts, Gorz could see no solution in which he could feel in accordance with his mother's demands and with himself. Subsequently he soon felt that the role of being her son was beyond his capacities.

Unable to identify with an ego so unrealistic that he could not adopt and develop it as his own, Gorz's recollections of this period have invited comparison with what the radical psychiatrist, R.D. Laing, termed 'ontological insecurity'.[56] Condemned for not conforming to his being-for-others, and subsequently feeling guilty and in danger of abandonment, he sensed that in order to come into possession of his own ego he had to somehow *deserve* it. But sensing his mother's displeasure, and the fact that he was probably less loved than his golden-haired sister, he felt incapable of competing for parental favours. In short, he was in danger of losing his sense of identity, value and orientation in the world:

> deprived of being, reduced to his inner shadows, he experienced a kind of catastrophic landslide – the universe collapsed, he fell into an abyss; his body was being stripped of his conforming and protecting identity, reducing itself to a heap of guilty flesh; self-conscious, virtually annihilated by his failure, he retired into a corner and longed for death.[57]

Finding himself within a situation which was beyond his means and comprehension, Gorz believes that his response was to make a 'prepersonal choice of nullity'. 'In the belief that in order to improve he would have to become *Other*...' and regulate his behaviour according to alien criteria, this effectively transfigured the repressive nature of his upbringing into infantile complexes characterised by a masochistic orientation towards himself and a terror of identification.

Gorz's theory of self

In accounting for the infantile development of his habits, character and affectivity towards the world, 'Gorz concedes that the child is an almost entirely conditioned social being',[58] and therefore absolves himself of all culpability:

> I am quite willing to assume all responsibilities, but not of the child I was made into ... Under given conditions a child of two or three is necessarily the way he is, and anyone would be the same in his place.[59]

In this respect, Gorz's self-analysis is clearly existentialist. Existence is seen to precede essence, with man initially existing as nothing, defining himself later. Furthermore, for Gorz, it is as a non-acting child, where there is 'neither history nor conscious practice nor the possibility of reflective consciousness' that one's original choice is made:

> For the child, it was entirely a question of conforming to the laws, the norms and the uncomprehended, alien, absolute orders governing his existence from without ... He receives *en bloc*, as a given value, the entire objective spirit of the society and is assigned the task of adapting himself to it ... even before he can have understood it, before he can establish himself within its reality as praxis.[60]

Significantly, it is upon this basis that Gorz disregards the Marxist 'ethic of doing' as a means of understanding childhood complexes. The emphasis placed upon questions of action, choice and responsibility within this theory are, he claims, wholly inappropriate when applied to the preconscious child. What are, for adults, problems of praxis to be resolved through action, are still, for a child, ontological issues orientated around knowing what one is and ought to be. Of greater relevance in determining the character of the child's original choice is

> whether the language which you are, in fact, for other people, is revealed as your power over them or as their power over you, as your possibility of manifesting yourself in the intersubjective universe of speech, or as your fall into the *other people's* universe of discourse.[61]

For Gorz, each child inevitably interiorises the requirement to identify itself from the ego presented within a matrix of symbolic discourses. What is crucial, however, is whether the ego presented corresponds to the child's real possibilities, or can only be achieved by assuming a false role. Ultimately, whether the child is loved, guided and encouraged to take charge of its alien self, rather than having it imposed upon them as an instrument of subjection and silence, is considered to be of the greatest significance.[62]

In Gorz's own case, because the latter possibility was clearly predominant, he developed 'a terror of being identified by other people with an ego that is an Other, a terror of saying more than he means, consequently a terror of saying anything at all'.[63] Lacking the ability either to be what his parents wanted him to be, or to rebel against their expectations, he concluded that the most worthy way of avoiding moral condemnation was to punish himself first.

Having accounted for the development of his original relationship to himself, others and the world, Gorz concerns himself with examining 'the "miraculous coincidence" between his infantile complexes, his "immemorial taste for annihilation" and the objective conditions of nullity he encountered as a young adult'.[64] It is an undertaking which, for Gorz, immediately evokes Western philosophy's original and most disturbing question.[65] It is also a venture in which Gorz's existential grounding becomes increasingly evident.

While Gorz maintains that the child's original choice is determined by the frame of their first conditioning, he claims that the extent to which this choice is enduring is largely dependent upon the individual. In a manner consistent with existential phenomenology, Gorz argues that one's subjective perceptions depend upon a preexistent element of choice. As such, as the individual grows older, they become capable of modifying the instruments of their perception to the changing circumstances around them. This ability for modification and initiative provides the potential for an existential conversion founded upon the ubiquitous presence of human freedom. Significantly, it is the failure to acknowledge the existence and potential of freedom as a basis for human action which leads Gorz to refute deterministic explanations in accounting for his personal history:

> The supposed conflict between the materialist explanation and psychoanalysis is a false dilemma. Both, although on different levels, explain man by his condition (material, infantile) ... This explanation is always true, but that is also its weakness; since every choice is conditioned, you can always prove it was 'given in advance' as a possibility ... but you can never prove it was fatal or necessary, or foresee it.[66]

What cannot be explained in terms of present or past conditioning alone, however, is that an individual should cling to instruments of perception which have their basis in the past and may be inappropriate for the contemporary reality. When such attitudes are maintained, Gorz argues, it is because we are afraid of sinking into nothingness if we fail to adhere to them.[67] Implicit in this view is the existentialist principle that the individual is ultimately responsible for what they become, with the human condition a product of man's own work.

> For man adapts himself to his condition only insofar as the fact of living it has founded a choice which gives it value, a choice occasioned or awakened by 'complexes' which cause him to feel comfortable in that condition, resigned to it, or proud of it.[68]

Within this process the individual may employ attitudes and values acquired during childhood in such a way that they seem necessary within the present. This is not simply a question of regressing to an infantile condition, because in making their choice the individual invests the complex with new significations, enabling it to grow. As such, in contrast to the psychoanalytic explanation, the original complex does not remain as a static, raw determinant which survives within the individual. On the contrary, it is presented as an actively developing phenomenon, drawing upon ever new meanings within the present.

> If the original complex survives instead of falling into oblivion with the rest of our childish attitudes, it can only do so to the degree that it has become much more than the original complex it was at the start. It is not the *attitude* of the child's original non-identification in relation to his mother which is perpetuating itself, but a *project* of nonidentification which discovers in events forever new reasons for development, forever new possibilities for refusing identification, and forever new significations for this refusal.[69]

With Gorz's emphasis upon human freedom, we can see that rather than the past exclusively conditioning the present and the future, the present and the future can also act upon the past, giving it variable significations. The extent to which this is the case will, however, inevitably depend upon the extent to which the individual assumes responsibility for their life, developing instruments of perception which reveal the most valuable potentialities at a given time. *The Traitor* provides a good example of this process, with Gorz recognising that in the past he had routinely exploited objective conditions of nullity to enrich his infantile complexes with significations no longer infantile. Rather than simply being a victim of a world which continued to reject him, his self-perception therefore changed to accommodate the fact that he had been an active and consistent collaborator with his own exclusion.[70]

Refusing identity

At the age of seven, Gorz recalls, his infantile 'failure' to establish a coherent sense of identity was exacerbated by the discovery of his mixed parentage and, in particular, his Semitic origins. Within a climate of increasing racial intolerance, the revelation of his Jewish blood came as a considerable shock. However, Gorz reasons, the significance that he attributed to this event was only explicable in the way that it served to justify his original choice of nullity. Having already placed himself within a position of inferiority, he responded to racism by investing it with an unfounded value. In the belief that his condition was already an enduring one, he was receptive to the derision of others, considering it to be well-founded. Instead of dismissing his initial encounter with Nazism, he therefore chose to utilise it to account for his feelings of weakness and exclusion. Ultimately, he had exploited the occasion to the benefit of his pre-historic choice and at the expense of historical objectivity:

> He was not the victim of the event. The event was an occasion for him to victimise himself. Objectively a wrong was done him; but he had chosen this wrong subjectively. *He was an accomplice to this injustice.*[71]

The subsequent development of his original attitude enabled Gorz to 'account' for his nullity by employing the discovery of his Jewishness as a biological and metaphysical alibi. He reasoned that his situation was an inevitable consequence of a marriage which had only produced half a man. He was 'half Jew, half Aryan – two halves that would never make a whole'.[72] Concluding that 'he would have to get rid of one or the other',[73] he gradually came to attribute all of his perceived weaknesses to his Jewish blood, while aspiring to anything radiating with Aryan vitality.

If Gorz had permitted his infantile complexes to mature in such a way as to instil a dichotomy at the very heart of his being, this development provided a further basis upon which to discover new possibilities for refusing identification in the future. The discovery of his mixed parentage had also served as a precedent for Gorz to become increasingly sensitive to the internal divisions within his family. It seemed that he was consistently being positioned between contradictory significations and truths, 'continually having to contest his father by his mother, his Jewishness by his Catholicism, his Catholicism by his Jewishness'.[74] This, in turn, undermined an already precarious relationship with the outside world by intensifying the belief that his home life lacked any stable foundation. With each moment apparently referring to its opposite, he arrived at the assumption that nothing in this life could be taken for granted.

At this point we can clearly identify, in embryonic form, the 'terror of identification' which characterised Gorz's condition of nullity during his adulthood. Having internalised the divisions within his own family, he believed that there was no role through which this 'half-caste' could effectively signify himself or escape contradiction. He was certainly tempted by all of the roles that the world had to offer, but he also felt unable to commit himself to any of them. On the contrary, he *chose* to persistently contest any course of action that he undertook, perpetuating the tendency to observe himself living a shallow and unhappy existence.

Self-negation

Feeling impotent in his search for a course of action in which he could affirm and reconcile himself, Gorz embarked upon a series of projects characterised by their austere self-discipline. Desperately seeking to overcome his sense of inferiority, but believing that this was only possible by overcoming himself, he sought a 'metaphysical metamorphosis' by employing an ascetic will upon his own being.

At the age of twelve, Gorz looked to a puritanical Catholicism to provide the miracle of his 'impossible transfiguration'. Incapable of accepting himself for what he was, and equally unable to satisfy the expectations of those around him, his religious conversion constituted an attempt to gain divine favour by adhering to the alien norms and values of an institutionalised faith. It was a choice which was made in the slender hope of an intangible self-emancipation. However, by virtue of its voluntaristic and gratuitous character, it was a choice which, conversely, could only serve to confirm him within his original attitude.

Projecting his own self-hatred upon the judgement of God, Gorz's faith was characterised by 'abjection, fear and trembling'. Before the omniscient presence of the Almighty, his persistent sense of guilt, and corresponding fear of punishment, manifested themselves as if the very fact of being himself was an act of the greatest sacrilege. In order to transcend these feelings, and ultimately achieve 'salvation', he would have to transcend himself and become *Other*. Attributing value to that which was most alien to him, the logic of his original attitude at once reflected his own minimal sense of worth, while encouraging a further self-debasement. Imposing an intransigent discipline upon himself which consisted of systematically doing 'the opposite of whatever he was spontaneously inclined to do', Gorz offered 'to God the pleasures he refused himself'.[75] In doing so, his brief flirtation with mysticism assumed the form of a physical and religious ascesis in which his project of nonidentification was inevitably perpetuated. Indeed, this was precisely the source of its interest and appeal in the first place.

Religion had, in fact, only aroused Gorz's curiosity from the moment that he discovered that it was a means of cancelling other people out. Furnishing him with demands which were far more severe than the expectations of his parents, it became the source of a pseudo-liberation, rendering the criticisms of others impotent. In this respect the judgement of God, even if it was terrible, protected him against the judgement of his fellow beings. In seeking to escape persecution he therefore negated and took flight from the affective reality by replacing it with an abstract counterpart. He had chosen 'to answer for requirements not personally intended for him, in order to conceal his failure to satisfy those which were'.[76]

This inclination toward contradictory signification, evident within each of Gorz's attempts at personal transformation, represented the practical expression of his fear of being identified with his acts. As the kernel of the 'treason complex' that he was unwittingly seeking to overcome, this manifested itself in the desire

> to disguise himself in a borrowed being which made no attempt to fool anyone, to mask his nullity by an Otherness which frankly admitted itself as such, to overcome his fellow beings, absolutely this time, on grounds completely alien to them (as to himself) ... A choice therefore of grounds upon which he was unbeatable because nobody dreamed of competing with him.[77]

The attraction of this tendency derived from the paradoxical combination of its masochistic and pseudo-emancipatory elements. Priding himself upon his extraordinary capacity for self-sacrifice, these not only provided him with an escape from the expectations of other people, but also became the basis of a unique, if ill-founded, dignity and freedom. For having 'stripped himself of everything that others clung to, he had conquered in himself the humanity by which they remained enslaved'.[78] With this statement the fundamental motivation belying Gorz's religiosity is finally revealed:

> Not to be here: to be only a transparent, ineffable and therefore invulnerable presence, a transcendent scrutiny sliding over the surfaces of events without taking hold, impervious to reproaches, disengaged from all commitments because absolutely committed to the absolutely Other – this is how he began his twelfth year, this is how he still is today.[79]

At the age of thirteen, influenced by his relationship with a Nazi pederast, Gorz abruptly substituted for Catholicism a glorified religion of strength and racial purity. Under the guise of a new antidote for his abhorrent imperfections, Gorz's identification with Nazism provided a further occasion for self-victimisation and the development of his fundamental attitude of refusal:

> To be a Nazi was, for him, to be something so absolutely Other that to possess even the barest trace of their vital values was to triumph over his abjection. For the young Gorz to succeed in becoming a Nazi would be to surpass all those who complacently believed in their Aryan essence: he would be the 'first amongst the last'.[80]

Seamlessly exchanging the role of the believer for that of the traitor, Gorz once again adopted the role of an intransigent discipline in favour of the concrete reality. Adhering to perfunctory routines in the name of an abstract universal, he continued to exact revenge upon human collectivities by betraying and renouncing them. More specifically, as the natural progression of a process which had begun with the discovery of his Jewish origins, Nazism was a choice in which he was able to simultaneously negate himself, his nation and, in particular, his parental upbringing:

> Strong, noisy and virile, the Nazis were the antithesis of the mediocrity, thrift, the pastoral honesty and petty narrow-mindedness of his Jewish father, whilst their law was more grand, impersonal and severe than the requirements imposed upon him by his mother.[81]

Nevertheless, as Bowring observes, the irony belying this futile act of rebellion was the fact that

> Gorz's original complex, his spontaneous, prefabricated attitude of nullity, guilt and inferiority, while only retrospectively attributed to his Jewishness, was actually nurtured by his mother's consuming endeavour to surmount the contradiction between her aristocratic ambitions and her Jewish husband by bringing forth a radiant super-Aryan son.[82]

Choosing abstraction

Repressing his 'inferior', spontaneous intuitions for standardised, spiritually purifying routines, Gorz had in each case endeavoured to supplant the activity of living with the obligation to obey fixed and unquestionable requirements. He had sought to relinquish responsibility for his own actions and, within this process, had abandoned the possibility of realising the human world of which he was part. In short, he had tried to mechanise his very existence, reducing to a minimum his lived contact with reality, 'in order to avoid the conflicts, contradictions and anguish which the slightest crack in his carapace of routines produces'.[83]

By employing these strategies to desert the constraints of others, the nature of these enterprises themselves ultimately remained exterior to him, serving to reinforce, rather than transform the profound basis of his choice. Because Gorz's every act was essentially an escape, voluntaristic in its nature and devoid of any real, internal necessity, he could not recognise himself in his actions. On the contrary, these became the source of a separation in which he could only project himself by virtue of 'a rational will hardened against itself'. The more he strived to aspire to these alien criterion, the more mediocre Gorz felt, lacking any conviction in the solidity of his role or himself. The bad faith which characterised his choices therefore served only to exacerbate his condition of alienation, perpetuating his infantile feelings of guilt, inferiority and exclusion. Indeed, it is in this respect that we can appreciate their transitory and ineffectual qualities, while recognising that their underlying motivations ensured that the desire towards difference and inauthenticity would remain a dominant theme into his adulthood.

Gorz's affinity with Nazism was involuntarily severed as Austria came under the control of the Reich. With violence and intimidation escalating against the Jewish community, the Nazis ascribed to Gorz the obscurely privileged status of a 'half-caste of the first class' because of his Catholic status. In the eyes of the fascists, it seemed, Gorz really was the 'first amongst the last'. Nevertheless, parental fears understandably intensified when, in order to make way for German dignitaries, the family was suddenly evicted from their apartment. With physical violence against Gorz and his family becoming a real threat, Gorz's indentification with the Nazis was finally broken.

Arriving in Switzerland on the eve of the Second World War, his 'second exile' rekindled the full force of his primary alienation. Reinforcing the abiding belief that his social exclusion and nullity would be the enduring features of his existence, Gorz's memories of being a child persecuted and threatened with abandonment undermined his motivation to resist and transform his conditions of exile. He was neglected rather than mistreated, but bereft of a coherent identity to defend, his resistance was further undermined as the pride of defiance was denied him.[84]

Feeling 'deeply sad and nostalgic for love, tenderness, and consolation for his inner suffering',[85] Gorz concentrated his energies upon his studies for the first time in his life. Initially attracted to the aridity of the natural sciences, he was tempted to reconstitute his treason complex by exchanging religious discipline for the impersonal Reason of science. By seeing the world scientifically, he postulated, he could effectively detach and intellectualise his affective contact with it, killing off its significations and playing dead. However, ultimately frustrated by the absence of a law through which he could mechanise the whole world and submit himself in servile obedience, he invented something else. He resolved to make himself French.

Abandoning the 'swamps of Teutonism' for his most radical discipline yet, Gorz turned to 'the Other of all that he was and knew, the Unknown par excellence', in order to lose himself once more.[86] Having disavowed his family, the Jews, the church, Austria and the Reich, 'he finally disavowed his mother tongue in order to become what he was least of all'.[87] Determining that the 'whole man' was now French; that the French language constituted the body of true thought, and that within France the good life still prevailed, Gorz resolved to expel from himself 'everything by which he was Other than the Other'.[88] It was a complete repudiation of everything that he was, everywhere that he had been, and everything that he could be.

Methodically reading his way through the French authors of any interest in the school library, Gorz laboriously assimilated French language and culture until, in direct contradiction to himself and his surroundings, 'he was thinking and dreaming in a language of otherness'.[89] Assuming the form of an 'autodestructive abstraction', he had acquired the French language as he had previously prayed, humbling himself before the superiority of French thought and the Reason that it bestowed. Returning to his original masochism, his French conversion therefore contained the same moral structure as the mystical crisis of four years before:

> Faced with the French absolute, he was nothing, a little fool struggling in the shadows ... Absolutely inferior because he was irremediably non-French, but in the very frame of this inferiority, the first among the non-French because he knew the inferiority others were unaware of and considered it with horror. How reassuring this religious universe was that he created for himself out of nothing.[90]

Gorz had by now assumed his condition of inferiority to such a degree that he spontaneously reinvented it whenever it was tending to modify itself. To privilege France as an absolute good enabled him to maintain his disgust of the world around him with a clear conscience. Convinced that the world was made by and for superior men, he had effectively relinquished the responsibility of realising his freedom and seeking to change his conditions. Rather than claiming humanity for himself, assuming his claims to be the basis of a justice he intended to demand, he had instead chosen to project it upon a nation which appeared to be the antithesis of himself. Feeling comfortable and secure in his status as a victim, he had ultimately chosen perpetual servitude in order to maintain it.

Following the same self-destructive logic, rather than serving to fracture his identification with the country, the fall of France to Germany became the basis of its intensification. Recognising that to love France was now to love that which did not exist, a choice which starkly revealed his affirmation of nonbeing against being, Gorz's association suddenly took on a new meaning:

> He who does not exist, who is only a nullity rejected by the world and without any possibility save to reject the world in return, suddenly has a brother, and this brother is a whole people, a nation annihilated like himself, existing no more than the dream by which he declares himself against the real machine. France is suddenly a brother in whom he recognises himself.[91]

Convinced that the French represented his own adventure transposed on to the scale of history, Gorz thought that to speak, read and think in French became an act of historical defiance. By the age of sixteen, persisting with attempts to escape his Austro-German/Judaeo-Christian contradictions, the prospect of surmounting his nullity complex through the myth of the French absolute had progressed to the act of writing.

Writing: self-negation and self-reconciliation

Gorz did not begin to write with the intention of becoming an author, in the belief that through the act of literary creation he might become someone. Instead, his writing was initially alienated, simply a further means of prayer and imitation. Disregarding his own thoughts and feelings as worthless, 'he wrote to learn the linguistic substance of other people's truth, in the hope that, ... by speaking as they did, he too would have true thoughts and feelings – theirs'. Attempting to forge himself a soul by virtue of values which essentially belonged to other people, Gorz began writing in order 'to get rid of himself'. And because he could only become true for himself by transposing himself in writing, it seemed that he was condemned to continue this elusive quest for truth and selfhood ad infinitum. However, in 1941, following a chance discovery of Sartre's *Nausea* and *The Wall*, Gorz was immediately struck by the revelatory confirmation of his own ontological despair. Recognising 'his' existence in the words of another, Gorz's lived experience was at last vindicated, precipitating the recognition that he was capable of a certain truth after all. From this point onwards he proceeded to contradict the significance of this literary affirmation by articulating his experience in purely Sartrian terms, deflecting it from its primary meaning in the hope of becoming a man like Sartre. Nevertheless, the realisation that these literary texts had provoked was significant in nurturing Gorz's resolve to write a philosophical treatise once he had completed his studies.

For several years to come, Gorz's philosophical endeavours would reveal, above all else, his consuming passion for negation.[92] On the one hand, he wrote in order to contest the world and everything within it, seeking to capture the absurdity, meaninglessness and contingency of life, on the other, in emphasising the pointlessness of writing about the futility of things, his critique destructively turned back on itself, negating the very basis of its own justification. It was a vain attempt to escape the absurdity of life by nullifying it in the abstract. It is therefore ironic that this 'concerted enterprise of annihilation' should have provided a basis for Gorz's belated engagement with the world.

Through the process of interrogating and articulating his contempt for each attitude and particularity, Gorz gradually developed a concrete interest in humanity which had previously been notable by its absence. And while this may have originally derived from nothing more than 'a parasitic hunger to make sense of other people's miseries',[93] it represented a slender thread linking him to reality. Coinciding with the discovery of an unfamiliar sense of agency and efficacy, in which the act of writing at last approximated the role of a means towards self-justification, in 1945 Gorz began rewriting *Fondements pour une morale*; this time in the vaguely optimistic belief that 'thought even when it tries to be the negation of everything, is a means of access to the universal, is universal itself provided it is coherent'.[94]

The turning of the tide

Gorz's hesitant rapprochement with humanity was enhanced by three significant events.[95] The first of these, in June 1946, was his initial meeting with Jean-Paul Sartre. Invited to attend Sartre's lecture in Lausanne by virtue of his comprehensive familiarity with his work, Gorz approached and monopolised his idol for several hours afterwards. Having elevated the philosopher to the status of a god, he was initially surprised by Sartre's 'oddly concrete look', precipitating the confusing realisation that he was only a man after all. However, Gorz's enduring recollection of the encounter was the recognition that, contrary to both his expectations and his own orientation towards the world, Sartre had a fundamental love of life and a horror of abstract ideas.

> For him, philosophy had to correspond to a search, a personal need, in order to contain an ounce of truth, and it was this search by which a man tries to create a path for himself that interested him, and not the fact that a man wrote or thought skilfully.[96]

When they met again in a Geneva bistro one week later, the fundamental difference in their approach to life and philosophy came to a head. Introducing his own ethic of being into the debate,[97] Gorz challenged Sartre, 'insisting that, since every choice the individual makes is unjustifiable, there is no meaningful preference for choice over abstention, for resistance over collusion'.[98] It was an attitude of existential nihilism which simultaneously revealed Gorz's hatred of everything that determined man, and his love of everything which negated that determination. Even so, he was hurt when Sartre perceptively replied that he seemed to be rather essentialist, despising the concrete.[99] It was a remark which encouraged Gorz's resolve to change, but left the enduring problem of what he could commit himself to unresolved.

The historical context of these meetings was nevertheless important in investing Gorz's writing with a new and concrete significance. While still living in Switzerland, he was mentally focused on a Paris at last freed from the Nazi occupation and beginning 'to explore the causes and the legacy of its loss of autonomy and integrity'.[100] It was an intellectual climate exploding with ideas, 'the great period' as Gorz refers to it, in which, because people felt that they were making a fresh start, it seemed that 'everything was possible'.[101] Inspired by the writings of Sartre, de Beauvoir, Merleau-Ponty and Jeanson, it seemed to Gorz that, within this context, intellectual speculation was afforded an elevated status and an objective meaning. He came to recognise that writing could represent an action, a constituent element of reality, rather than simply its sterile negation.

The second influential episode in Gorz's improving situation related to the changing character of his interactions with others and its subsequent implications on his approach to philosophy and life. Since embarking on his philosophical sojourn, his relations with others had continued in a distant and remote vein. Taking refuge within the realm of ideas, his interactions were undermined from the outset by his strict adherence to the abstract, a priori principles through which he effectively concealed and protected himself. Choosing unilateral, rather than reciprocal relationships, his acquaintances were of interest to him only to the extent that they could be observed and provide contingent examples supporting his general theory. Towards this end they represented little more than objects subjected to psychoanalysis and categorisation within his hierarchy of human attitudes.

However, in November 1946, the termination of an ill-fated relationship provoked the dawning awareness of the importance of human beings over the abstract mind, and of love as a means of transcending alienation. This revelation was consolidated shortly afterwards when, having met 'Kay', his future wife, he finally had to make a choice between the woman he loved and his beloved philosophical principles. In this fateful moment 'he discovered that principles were after all, from the moment that he was the only one to defend them, not so important, since they were now identified with his will as an individual quarrelling with another will'.[102]

When Gorz pledged himself to 'Kay' in the spring of 1948, he did so in the modest acknowledgement that making life liveable for another person might be the only concrete undertaking he would ever accomplish.[103] He had discovered that he could no longer live as if he did not exist, attempting to accommodate the conflicting demands of being a pure, disembodied consciousness and a human being at the same time. And he had recognised that his intransigent devotion to a priori thinking had been nothing more than a refusal of real existence, an additional betrayal of himself. In short, he had acted in the conviction that it was worth more to be a 'living' man, with the inevitable compromises and contradictions that this entailed, than the coward and the traitor that he would have remained as an uncompromising and 'dead' philosopher. After all, he reasoned,

> What use is it to have universal ideas in the abstract if these ideas prevent you from being a man, even if only in the eyes of a single person, and if in their name you refuse yourself and to another person what can make life liveable?[104]

In the spring of 1947, the opportunity to write articles for a leftist weekly had provided the catalyst for the third significant feature of Gorz's self-reconciliation: 'the discovery of reality through journalism'.[105] In his role as a political journalist, Gorz found himself increasingly stimulated by contemporary events and realities which would have previously appeared insignificant. With his work finally validated by the recognition of a regular readership, reporting on the issues and struggles of his time gradually became the source of a new meaning and awareness. In particular, by intellectually engaging with the contingent realities of everyday life, Gorz would ultimately come to recognise that the world was not constituted in a manner enabling freedom to use it creatively as a means towards self-realisation.[106] It was a discovery which would have considerable implications for both the man and his work.

'I'

In the 1940s, André Gorz had embarked upon *Fondements pour une morale* in the belief that he was producing 'a tool for thinking oneself into being'.[107] At that time he was convinced that, through a careful analysis and assumption of one's factual position, an individual could successfully seek to transform themselves and their situation. In other words, he believed 'that individuals changed their lives and the world through mental activity'.[108]

In their respective concerns to develop and assume a self-analysis appropriate to the existential conversion, both *Fondements* and *The Traitor* represent a practical expression of this conviction. Like the work of the early Sartre, the aims and methods employed within these texts reflect a confidence in the ontological liberty of humankind and a refutation of determinisms to the contrary. However while, for Gorz, the tendency to universalise human freedom did not preclude a recognition of the social dimensions of alienation,[109] the emphasis afforded to the individual consciousness did have a number of important consequences. In particular, it would appear that the possibility of *collectively* transforming the limitations that the constituted praxis held for the expression of freedom remained, for the most part, unarticulated. Indeed, this is evident in the absence of a comprehensive theory of intersubjectivity. However, in the final chapter of *The Traitor* it is evident that Gorz's recognition of his 'project on nonidentification' heralded a new way of seeing and being in the world, with important consequences for the future direction of his work. Entitled 'I' in order to reflect his discovery of a basis for self-affirmation, it is here that Gorz speaks of himself in the first person for the first time. Significantly, in a manner which prefigures Gorz's shift from existential philosophy towards an existential Marxism, the chapter begins with a reference to Marx, proclaiming that 'what consciousness does in isolation is ... without the slightest interest'.[110]

Having completed his self-analysis, Gorz concedes that

> I no longer believe, as at the outset of this work, that a man can change radically, can liquidate his original choice. But I am now convinced that by a careful analysis of his empirical situation, he can discover in his choice potential objective significations that permit him to reach positive conclusions.[111]

In this respect, while it is evident that Gorz now considers a 'conversion' approximating his original intentions to be unfeasible, he also believes it to be beyond the realms of practical expediency:

> This is the whole question. You are never asked to change yourself altogether, but to learn to employ your resources, with full knowledge of the case, in view of a positive action (if you prefer, to learn to make use of what you are in order to transcend yourself). This is the point I have reached.[112]

Having identified his complex of nonidentification, Gorz reveals that it has subsequently 'drained like an abscess'. He has been able to perceive its original meaning in a new and less oppressive light, enabling him to interact in a more open and spontaneous manner. In particular, his fear of the incongruous reactions of others has diminished, creating the basis for a new affective relationship with the world:

> Instead of keeping the world at a distance like an enemy who must not be allowed to get a grip on me, I am learning to yield to it; to see it, to begin with, to taste its density, my presence within it, ... to be able to enjoy the passing moment, a light, an aroma, a look, a sound; to hold on to life, to want it to be full of all there is to be lived, including contradictions and risks that cannot be escaped – I am learning.[113]

As such, while it is clear that the outcome of this uniquely personal philosophical enterprise is not exactly as Gorz would have anticipated, we may conclude that it was ultimately successful in re-establishing Gorz's 'taste for the concrete'. Furthermore, his increasingly enthusiastic engagement with the world would provide the basis for a new direction in his thought.[114] In *The Traitor*, this shift is indicated when, having identified the subjective sources of his alienation, Gorz states that he no longer considers such individual motivations to be so important.[115] This implicit acknowledgement of the social bases of alienation, and subsequently of the individual's powerlessness to transform them in isolation, announces a greater emphasis upon why 'the development of one's own freedom is rendered impossible by the actual situation, and what determines this?'[116] In this respect, while freedom would remain both a fact and a goal within Gorz's writings, his enduring concern to explore the conditions of the possible achievement of the goal would result in an increasingly political dimension to his work. Indeed, even as Gorz proclaims his identification and solidarity with the oppressed in the concluding chapter of the text, it is evident that, for him, the overcoming of alienation now *depended* on collective organisation and action.

The Socialism of the Early Gorz

In the mid-1950s Gorz wrote:

> This much is certain: that I am on one side (the side of those who do not have enough to know they are a side), that I have no possibility of changing sides, that I will not change even if they try to buy me for the other side because it is 'really' my own, and that the other side will always be the *other* side ... I am on the side of those who have ... only their own strength, which consists of ruse, bluff and the capacity to take advantage of its own weaknesses.[1]

Gorz is also certain that

> the intellectual, if he cannot keep from being one, is objectively on the side of the revolutionary forces, of historical negativity, and he must be on that side subjectively. This is the intellectual's only chance of reality. In isolation he can do nothing.[2]

Gorz's commitment to the struggle for socialism never wavers. At the same time however it is a commitment that respects the autonomy of all individuals. As such Gorz's socialism is at odds with the prevailing socialist orthodoxies of the time. Gorz made this clear in *La Morale de l'histoire*.[3] But Gorz's commitment to socialism is not restricted to the limited intellectual project of theory. In Gorz theory is always practically oriented. This enables him to avoid the self-indulgences of academic excess, and at the same time, to infuse his writing with a political urgency rarely found in theoretically informed texts.

In his role as economics editor of *Les Temps Modernes* and in his articles for the socialist weekly, *Le Nouvel Observateur*, Gorz's writings were both influential and inspirational for a growing number of student activists in the 1960s.[4] By the time he published *Strategy for Labour* in 1964, Gorz's commitment to the struggle for socialism had led him to address the most difficult question facing the left at this time: how do we develop socialism in the midst of increasing affluence? In this chapter we will follow Gorz's thinking in relation to this question, primarily by concentrating on his two main political texts of the 1960s – *Strategy for Labour* and *Socialism and Revolution*.[5] Later in this chapter we will also draw on his studies of the division of labour, which as we shall see in the next chapter, gradually led Gorz to reconsider the focus of his strategy for emancipatory social change.

In *Strategy for Labour* Gorz accepted that the working class could no longer be characterised in terms that were appropriate for an earlier era. A number of sociologists in the United States and Europe had studied the changing internal structure and composition of the working class. Particular attention was focused on the growing affluence of the working class, and the relationship between this and their political allegiances and willingness (or lack of it) to participate in militant action.[6] A number of left-wing intellectuals became increasingly dismissive of the revolutionary potential of the working class. Sartre, for example, fell into this camp. By the end of the 1950s Sartre began to place his hopes in the revolutionary potential of anti-imperialist movements in the Third World. Gorz tells us that '*Strategy for Labour* was my reply to his [Sartre's] dismissal of the possibility of revolution in the industrial metropolis'.[7] As we shall see Gorz argued that the increasing affluence and fragmentation of the working class were real enough but did not tell the full story. The road to affluence was accompanied by new forms of poverty, and workers' alienation and the frustration of their qualitative or existential needs suggested a basis of common interests.

Important too in Gorz's optimism were the signs of an anti-capitalist sensibility which was emerging throughout the Western world. Gorz, particularly through his journalism, played some part in stimulating this sensibility, which tended to embrace 'gut' rejection of US imperialism, of the exploitative character of capitalism, of the authority of the state and the values it represented. It identified itself with persecuted minorities in the advanced capitalist societies, and with the oppressed majorities in the Third World. It campaigned and protested for peace, equality, justice and freedom. While this new sensibility was largely confined to the younger sections of society, particularly students, Gorz was hopeful that it would spread into workers' organisations. There were indications that this was happening among young workers. On top of this, politicised students do enter the labour force.

Part of the new sensibility was a growing disillusionment with the socialism of the Soviet Union. This disillusionment had swelled as a consequence of the Soviet invasion of Hungary in 1956. Additionally many on the left were expressing serious concern about the totalitarian tendencies in Soviet society and their reflection in the authoritarianism institutionalised in communist parties in capitalist societies, and in the trade unions. Left critics (the New Left) of the Soviet-inspired left (the Old Left) had hinted at the need to develop a different kind of socialism – one that respected

human autonomy and creativity. While various alternative visions
of a socialist society found some expression among New Left
theorists, no one had indicated a feasible means of achieving
socialism.[8] Gorz filled this vacuum. As Arthur Hirsch observes,
Strategy for Labour 'was the most comprehensive statement of new
left political strategy to appear in the 1960s'.[9] It 'provided the basis
for the French new left's political strategy ... [and it won Gorz] ...
international recognition as a major strategist for a militant working
class movement'.[10] Had the activists of May 1968 paid closer
attention to the details of *Strategy for Labour*, subsequent events
would no doubt have been quite different.

Strategy for Labour, however, is far more than a text of the 1960s.
Mark Poster describes it as the 'best articulation of the meaning
of advanced capitalism for the working class'.[11] Gorz not only sets
out ways of achieving socialism, he provides the new sensibility with
much needed theoretical meat, and in his analysis of the manipulation
of needs in advanced capitalism he connects with the lived experience
of the vast majority in ways that disclose the roots of contemporary
frustrations. In our view, the continuing relevance of *Strategy for
Labour* and *Socialism and Revolution* resides in the pathbreaking
analysis of the manipulation of needs. This analysis provides the
basis of Gorz's critique of advanced capitalism, it informs his
critique of traditional left strategy, and it permeates his vision of
socialism and how it can be best achieved.

The manipulation of needs

Gorz recognises that 'in the advanced countries the revolt against
society has lost its *natural base*'. He reasons that 'as long as misery,
the lack of basic necessities, was the condition of the majority, the
need for a revolution could be regarded as obvious'.[12] Of course,
Gorz accepts that the basic needs of the majority in the Third World
are far from satisfied, and here the need for revolution is clear, but,
he argues, one cannot expect the most impoverished, those struggling
to survive, to become the driving force for emancipatory social
change. Rather the 'less poor sectors of the population' are the
potential agents of radical social change. In the Third World the
struggle for socialism will initially be driven by the need to satisfy
basic needs, but in the affluent societies the need for socialism arises
from 'qualitative needs'. By qualitative needs Gorz is referring to
the needs of creativity, communication and autonomy, in short,
the need for a meaningful life. Gorz believes that this need has
emerged among the vast majority in the advanced societies and
argues that 'the struggle for a meaningful life is the struggle against
the power of capital'.[13] As such the struggle for socialism in the

affluent societies is essential to the development of socialism in the Third World, 'imperialism cannot be beaten at its periphery unless it is also attacked at its centre, the metropolis itself'.[14] And it is the successful struggle against the power of capital that will eliminate poverty in the advanced societies.

One of the major obstacles in the way of the struggle for socialism is that qualitative needs are not always immediately obvious. When they are obvious, the means for their satisfaction are rarely available. *Strategy for Labour* attempts to render the need for socialism obvious by explaining the dissatisfactions and frustrations which are commonly experienced by the vast majority, and by describing the kinds of practices which can both expose these needs and reveal what has to be done to satisfy them. If qualitative needs 'are not easily perceived', if 'they can be repressed and blurred by propaganda, indoctrination, and fun into some vague feeling of dissatisfaction and emptiness', and if 'they have no spontaneous means of self-expression',[15] do they actually exist? Could they be a figment of Gorz's imagination? In response it can be argued that the need for a meaningful life is a universal need (there is more to life than mere self-reproduction, or at least there should be) and that it necessarily involves autonomy, creativity, communication, mutuality and so on. But Gorz does not depend on this kind of argument. He argues that 'to reveal deeply felt (but also hidden) needs and articulate them, *we first must show how their satisfaction is actually within our reach*'.[16] This remains important for Gorz. We must have a model of what is possible.

Capitalism, however, has pursued a path that is antithetical to the satisfaction of qualitative needs. Having provided the basic necessities for a majority in the advanced capitalist societies, instead of extending this provision to *all*, and instead of placing the productive forces at the disposal of 'human ends', capitalism generated a number of ways of preventing this. As Gorz suggests,

> individuals freed from natural necessity in theory arrive at the possibility of choosing the nature of the wealth to be produced, the possibility of producing for consciously creative human ends and no longer for natural human ends; the possibility of submitting the mode and the apparatus of production, as well as production itself, to the requirement of producing 'human men'; and finally, the possibility of concentrating essentially on creativity in production as well as in consumption.[17]

All of this is possible but, in fact, none of this has happened. Instead of qualitative needs being given a free reign, capitalism has devised new ways of maintaining its domination, and in the process ensures our enslavement to fundamental needs, creates new needs, and as a consequence further submerges qualitative needs. In short capitalism, in its pursuit of profit, and in its desire to maintain its domination, manipulates our needs.

Against the sociological fashion of the time, and in defiance of political propaganda, Gorz knows that the so-called growing affluence of the working class is contradicted by their experience. He explains this contradiction by pointing out that needs and 'desires are conditioned by the possibility of their fulfilment, in other words, by the general social conditions in which they arise'.[18] Gorz devotes considerable attention to how this applies to basic needs. These needs, Gorz argues, are not only

> conditioned by the development of the means available for their satisfaction. They are conditioned by the development of the techniques of production ... They are conditioned finally by the changes which the development of production techniques brings about in the natural environment, in the (ecological) relation of man to nature.[19]

Furthermore, 'industrial growth reveals or sharpens certain needs which had not previously been felt'.[20] Essentially basic needs are exploitable for profit. Gorz provides examples of how some basic necessities are to be satisfied by goods designed for unnecessary frequent purchase as a consequence of planned obsolescence, and examples of how 'the usefulness of an object becomes the *pretext* for selling superfluous things that are built into the product and multiply its price'.[21] Today this is most clearly illustrated in the manufacture of cars, articles of clothing and household appliances. These products, too, 'are sold above all for their packaging and brand names (that is to say, advertising), while their use value becomes a secondary part of the bargain'.[22]

All of this is familiar enough. It accounts, in part, for the common experience of having increases in income swallowed up by the rising costs of basic necessities. Additionally, however, basic necessities have expanded. This might normally be taken to mean that we have developed a 'need' for something that was once a luxury, or at least superfluous to need. But of greater relevance here is Gorz's analysis of how fundamental needs are modified as a consequence of the changing conditions under which we must reproduce ourselves. Industrialism, Gorz argues, has altered our relationship with nature and has replaced the natural environment with an ever-changing social environment. Gorz refers to the 'exhaustion or destruction of resources (air, water, light, silence, space) which until now were taken as natural'.[23] He shows how our need for these resources can only be satisfied by expensive purchases, often in a complex form.

This is true, for example, of the need for air, which is immediately apprehended as the need for vacations, for public gardens, for city planning, for escape from the city; of the need for nightly rest, for physical and mental relaxation, which becomes the need for tasteful, comfortable housing protected against noise.[24]

In these and other examples Gorz reminds us that

the need in question is not a new and 'rich' need which corresponds to an enrichment of man and a development of his faculties; it is merely an eternal biological need which now demands 'rich' means of satisfaction because the natural environment has become impoverished.[25]

Since Gorz wrote *Strategy for Labour* further changes in our social environment have increased the number of objects necessary for self-reproduction. For example, access to the use of a telephone has become a basic necessity, and numerous mutually reinforcing changes (in the food retail oligopolies, in food processing, public transport, housing developments, travel distances to food stores, and so on) have rendered the refrigerator essential. Arguably the most significant of the new necessities is the car. In the context of declining public transportation and urban sprawl, access to work, shops, recreational and cultural facilities requires private transportation. The effects of car pollution and the dangers created by the speed and density of traffic discourages the use of the bicycle. 'The private automobile becomes a social necessity', Gorz observes, because 'urban space is organised in terms of private transportation'.[26]

Gorz's explanation of the manipulation of needs is an integral part of his critique of capitalism. The capitalist state, Gorz argues, while maintaining a level of public expenditure – on health, education, welfare, and so on – sufficient to support the needs of major companies for skilled labour and a healthy workforce, actually diverts funds away from providing for collective needs. The capitalist state thus uses public money to support and work in concert with companies intent on producing for profit. In a real sense taxpayers are subsidising wasteful, unnecessary production. The car industry again provides a useful illustration of Gorz's argument.

For the production of a means of evasion and escape, this industry has diverted productive resources, labour, and capital from priority tasks such as housing, education, public transportation, public health, city planning, and rural services. The priority given by monopoly capitalism to the automobile gets stronger and stronger: city planning must be subordinated to the requirements of the automobile, roads are built instead of houses ... and public transportation is sacrificed.[27]

Collective needs can only be satisfactorily met collectively. But this runs counter to the logic of capitalism. Collective needs are either ignored or translated (more often than not unsatisfactorily) into facilities and services for individual purchase. The consumer, in a sense, is paying several times over for her or his impoverishment. The consumer pays taxes which provide major companies with the infrastructure (for example roads) they require for their profit-making practices. The consequences of the continuing search for more and more profit by incorporating unnecessary gimmicks and innovations in what is produced means that resources that could be of social use are wasted, and in the process the environment is impoverished by air and water pollution. The consumer thus lives in impoverished circumstances which can only be alleviated by purchasing goods, which, in turn, reproduces and reinforces the very system which created the need for the purchase in the first place.

> Hence the familiar spectacle, in America and Europe, of slums with televisions, shantytowns with private cars, homes with refrigerators but without bathrooms or running water, illiteracy with transistor sets. And it is not only in the semi-developed economies, but also in those that are highly developed, that monopolist expansion, instead of abolishing scarcity, merely shifts it to other levels.[28]

Gorz has demonstrated that the consumption patterns of the majority can be explained without recourse to ideas which demean the individual consumer. Gorz does not need to use the concept of 'false consciousness' with all its elitist pitfalls. Neither does he fall into the equally problematic trap of a cultural populism which sees consumerism as an enjoyable, and even satisfying, expression of autonomy. The reason why Gorz is able to achieve his particular understanding of consumption is his sensitivity to the lived experience of the majority. It is this sensitivity which enables Gorz to understand that the manipulation of needs arises from and reinforces the powerlessness of the individual. Thus Gorz concludes that 'the preferences for the priorities and the values of the "society of consumption" for the ideology of mature capitalism is ... not spontaneous; it arises out of the individual's powerlessness to define and to prefer something else'.[29] The individual's attempts to satisfy felt needs is restricted to 'acquiring the individual goods offered by the oligopolies'.[30]

It is Gorz's sensitivity, too, to the lived experience of the majority that enables him to understand alienated and manipulated consumption as having its source in the alienated work of the powerless worker.

The needs of 'affluent' consumption created by advanced capitalism are not wholly artificial. To a very great extent they are the needs of the crippled and frustrated worker who, being unable to find any interest or personal satisfaction in his work, falls easy prey during his leisure hours to the merchants of distraction and creature comfort, *private* compensations for the traumas inflicted on him by the social process.[31]

Thus 'so long as work continues to be destructive of the individual, a constraint and oppression which he is obliged to endure, the field of non-work will be the field of escape, distraction and passive enjoyment'.[32]

The alienation of labour for Gorz, it must be emphasised, is the source of the ways in which needs are manipulated. While production determines consumption, and while the motor of production is the pursuit of profit, work and workers will be subordinated to demands that are essentially dehumanising. It is in these circumstances, too, that workers have no control over what is produced and how it is produced.

The alienated consumer is one and the same as the manual, intellectual, or white collar worker who is cut off from his fellow workers made passive by the military discipline of the factory, cut off from his product, ordered to sell his time, to execute with docility a pre-fabricated task, without worrying about the purposes of his work.[33]

Gorz's analysis here is not original. As he acknowledges, he is 'paraphrasing Marx'. However the implications of this analysis of the source of the manipulation of needs for political strategy, as Gorz develops them, does place him at odds with the established strategy of the labour movement, and with the communist parties of the time. Gorz was very much aware of this. He knew that if his ideas were to have any impact in the struggle for socialism he would have to spell out why the existing conceptions of how the struggle for socialism should be conducted were inadequate.

Critique of Old Left strategies

As we have already noted, Gorz was highly critical of the Old Left's conception of socialism. He did, nevertheless, share with the revolutionary factions (as distinct from the reformist factions) of the Old Left a distrust of, and lack of faith in, those strategies which placed their hopes in a parliamentary route to socialism. Unless a government's 'clear resolve', Gorz maintains, 'is to wage a long, drawn-out battle, appealing to mass mobilisation and active popular support, with the aim of transferring economic power to the public (which may mean the State, but does not necessarily do so)', it cannot bring about socialism. The reason why this is so is that 'no government can afford to antagonise Big Business'.[34] In the early 1960s, and ever since, there has been no sign of a major left party, in the advanced capitalist societies, possessing the kind of resolve required to establish socialism. In the meantime the state has well and truly subordinated itself to the orientation of big business. Government has become an increasingly restricted sphere of influence. Political parties display only 'marginal differences' as they compete for posts already subservient to capital.

> Political competition, in these conditions, does not bring into play opposed concepts of policy and of the state but is simply concerned with different ways of implementing the same basic policy determined in advance by the existing balance of forces and social relations.[35]

As we shall see, even though Gorz has no time for the institutions of bourgeois democracy, he does not rule out the value of a mass party expressing the will of the people. Having said this it is obviously the case that Gorz is opposed to the elitist, vanguard role adopted by many revolutionary parties of the Old Left. The vanguard typically does not express the will of the majority, and if it just happens to be in touch with the experienced needs of the majority this will have occurred by chance. Of course, this is no basis for revolution. Again, as we shall see, the only vanguard which Gorz can accommodate in his strategy, is one with a specific function and a limited life.

Gorz has no truck, too, with those who predict the inevitable collapse of capitalism. This prediction is based on the belief that the internal contradictions of capitalism would sharpen, as capitalism plunges from crisis to crisis, and that as a consequence the suffering of the working class would be sufficient to impel them to seize power. This belief, widespread in the communist movement of the time, Gorz argues, generates fears that working-class struggles, if successful, 'will remove – or blunt for a long time – the workers' discontent and their revolutionary spirit', and 'will reinforce the system and render it more bearable'.[36] Rather than engage with workers' struggles, leaders of the communist movement were content to 'wait for the revolution', occasionally stoking 'the flames of revolutionary discontent'. Such a policy, Gorz observes, demonstrates a 'more or less pronounced inability to link the struggle for socialism to the everyday demands of the workers'.[37] This failure, and the attitude underpinning it

> leads to an impasse. Lacking perspectives and positive accomplishments, the revolutionary flame begins to dim. Certainly,

capitalism is incapable of fundamentally resolving the essential problems which its development has brought about. But capitalism can resolve these in its own way, by means of concessions and superficial repairs aimed at making the system socially tolerable.[38]

Waiting for the revolution, rather than intervening in workers' struggles to make it happen, enables capitalism to strengthen its position via more concessions.

The communist movement's non-interventionist policy was complemented by its silent acceptance of the model of development pursued in the Soviet Union. It was assumed that 'come the Revolution', the Soviet model of central planning and organisation would replace capitalism. In effect, it was not necessary to reflect on what a socialist society could become. The Soviet Union was the way forward. But herein resides a major problem. Gorz accepts that when the priority of socialist societies was that of satisfying basic needs central planning was necessary. The forces of production had to be harnessed to serve this priority, but in the process there emerged 'an ethic of productivity'. This is

> an ethic of self-denial, frugality, austerity, unremitting labour and self-discipline, and also of moral vigour, prudery, cleanliness and sexual repression. Man, according to this ethic, was not brought into this world to enjoy himself and cultivate his senses, but to surpass himself in his passion for work; he would reap his reward in the future society for the sake of which he was sacrificing the here and now.[39]

As a consequence, 'all those needs which were not directly productive – that is to say, whose satisfaction was not necessary to the reproduction or increase of labour power'[40] were backgrounded and censored. But the Soviet state gave insufficient consideration as to what to do when the productive forces were successfully meeting basic needs. In other words, very little attention was given to 'the *criteria* whereby the production of non-indispensable goods, their quantity, style and quality, is decided'.[41] As Gorz notes,

> In principle, under a socialist economy, these are matters that should be decided by the free choice of the associated producers ... [O]ne would expect this choice to be governed by an overall concept of the socialist civilisation yet to be created; by concern for the progressive enrichment of individual needs and therefore of the content of collective life, and for the progressive fulfilment of those needs by the growth of free social services and consumptions rather than individual ones – in a word by a coherent scale of priorities.[42]

In the absence of anything like this happening, and given the unpredictability and variable expressions of individual needs, it is hardly surprising that central planning proved to be inefficient and inadequate with respect to producing the non-essentials. Rather than providing an alternative, socialist model of production and consumption, the Soviet Union, in the main, imitated capitalism. While this invited comparisons with Western patterns of consumption – fuelling discontent among Soviet workers and a stronger productivist resolve among their leaders – it also meant that the Soviet worker was no less alienated in his or her labour than the worker in capitalist societies. And, while this alienation had been justified in times of scarcity, those times had passed, and with them the justification for the alienation of labour.

The communist movement in the capitalist societies was blind to the problems inherent in the alienation of labour both in capitalist and socialist societies. Hence its acceptance of the Soviet model as unproblematic, perhaps requiring some fine tuning only, and its insensitivity to workers' experience in capitalism. Given the causal role Gorz attributes to the alienation of labour in the manipulation of needs, we can readily appreciate why he was critical of the strategies of the Old Left. As we shall see later, this manipulation does have other dimensions.

Gorz's strategy

In view of the significance Gorz attaches to the alienation of labour it is not surprising that his political strategy is directed at reducing this alienation, and, in the process, establishing the prerequisites for the development of socialism. The kind of socialism favoured by Gorz is one in which the best conditions for the full expression of individual and collective freedom are created. The only way forward is through a process of collective self-determination. In other words, socialism cannot be handed to us on a plate – it is something that we make for ourselves, and in the process we experience and develop the autonomy and voluntary co-operation necessary to ensure the capability of continuing to shape social conditions in response to our needs.

This sounds fine, but what does it mean in practice? Essentially it means that we must fight for more autonomy. And, in societies in which work is the main social activity, it makes sense to fight for more autonomy in work. Opportunities for such a fight present themselves in labour disputes. But, it can be argued, surely most disputes are about wages. Is it not the case that workers can be pacified with a small increase in wages? Does this not suggest that consumer autonomy is more important to workers than autonomy in work? For a start, Gorz argues that

> wage demands are in fact a protest against ... the oppression of the worker, the systematic mutilation of his person, the stunting of his professional and human faculties, the subordination of the nature and content of his working life to a technological evolution deliberately hidden from his powers of initiative, of control, and even of anticipation ... Wage demands are more often motivated by a revolt against the workers' condition itself than against the rate of economic exploitation of labour power.[43]

Increases in wages cannot possibly match the motivations underpinning workers' protests. What these motivations do represent is an alienation that can only be successfully addressed by workers gaining autonomy. But under the conservative leadership of traditional trade unions, in which the economic rationality of capitalism is largely accepted, 'only the price of labour may be disputed with management ... not control over the conditions and nature of work'.[44]

The conservative unions restrict their sphere of influence to matters that can be readily accommodated by the capitalist system, and in which the bosses always have the final say. Increased labour costs are only very temporary – they are recouped by price rises and by reducing the labour force. The union, within this situation, is always on the *defensive* – fighting job cuts and balancing this need with an apologetic demand for more pay. Often this will be duly granted. Thus the cycle repeats itself continuously. In this context,

> even when highly paid, the worker has no choice but to sell his skin, and therefore he tries to sell it as dearly as possible. And inversely, no matter what price he receives for selling his liberty, that price will never be high enough to make up for the dead loss which he suffers in qualitative and human terms; even the highest pay will never restore to him control over his professional life and the liberty to determine his own condition.
>
> The simple wage demand thus appears as a distortion and a mystification of a deeper demand.[45]

This deeper demand – the reduction of alienation in work – can be met only by gaining more autonomy. This will remain an important theme for Gorz. As we shall see later, Gorz today believes that the best bet for reducing alienation in work is radically to reduce working hours. But in the 1960s, in the pre-micro-chip era, the most feasible way of reducing alienation in work was to *fight* for workers' control of work and work conditions. The latter 'include work speeds, wage differentials, the evaluation of skills and jobs, health and sanitary conditions, transportation to and from work, breaks, working hours, industrial organisation, the right of assembly on the spot, etc.'. As Gorz says, these 'things are within their [the workers'] reach and can be realised by their own direct actions'.[46] Of course, this is merely the beginning. Gorz is outlining what is possible and spells this out for levels of struggle other than the place of work.

> – On the company level, by the conquest of a workers' counter-power concerning the rate of profits, the volume and orientation of investments, technical level and evolution;
> – On the industry and sector level, by the *fight* against over investment, fraught with future crises; and the *fight* against the shortcomings of capitalist initiative as regards the development of socially necessary production; both *fights* having to be linked to a programme of industrial reorientation and/or reconversion.[47]

Similarly, Gorz provides examples of what is attainable by struggles at the levels of the city, the province, the nation, and Europe.

To his credit Gorz always attempts to link critique and theory to concrete examples. But what concerns us more here is not so much the content of the concrete examples reflecting Gorz's strategy for socialism, but the underlying principles of this strategy. The content, after all, will vary throughout time, and from place to place. The key principle in Gorz's strategy is that socialism, and the means of achieving it, must involve the expansion of individual and collective autonomy. Gaining autonomy, not only to reduce alienation in work, but to exercise control over all aspects of our lives, is the essence of Gorz's socialism. But the dominance of capitalism depends on restricting and confining individual and collective autonomy to activities which pose no threat to the system. Indeed, the system actually strengthens itself through such practices. Thus Gorz reminds us that 'Capital ... cannot perpetuate its domination unless the individual's need for autonomy and creativeness is repressed and diverted towards substitute activities and satisfactions, which capitalism readily offers and stimulates'.[48] And, it is precisely because this is the case that the expansion of individual and collective autonomy inevitably involves a struggle against the forces of capital. Capitalism will not relinquish its powers without a fight. This is why we have emphasised that significant gains in autonomy cannot be achieved without having to *fight* for the attainable. Gorz knows this only too well. Hence he refers to his strategy for the labour movement as an *aggressive* strategy. Socialism, Gorz insists,

> can be brought about only by deliberate, long-term action of which the *beginning* may be a scaled series of reforms, but which, as it unfolds, must grow into a series of trials of strength,

more or less violent, some won and others lost, but of which the outcome will be to mold and organise the socialist resolve and consciousness of the working classes.[49]

By 'reform', Gorz does not mean 'improvements' to the capitalist system which keep the system intact. Such improvements are 'reformist reforms', whereas Gorz is advocating anti-capitalist or 'revolutionary reforms'. These are reforms that modify the balance of power by gains in autonomy for those pushing from below. The value of revolutionary reforms for the labour movement resides as much in the *experience* of struggling for them as in the 'content' of the actual reform. Not only do workers or citizens encounter resistance from those in power – a resistance that often reveals vulnerabilities in the system which can be attacked – but the experience of the collective self-determination of struggle reveals capacities for self-rule. This experience is essential for laying the foundation for future struggles in so far as it begins to develop an ethos of participation or direct democracy necessary for forging the solidarity which is an integral ingredient of the resolve required to fight for more power. As Gorz argues, this experience prepares people 'to refuse domination by management and by the state as well as by party and union bureaucracies'.[50] Fighting for anti-capitalist reforms is thus the basis of the political self-education of workers and citizens. Successful struggles create the need for a further conquest of power. 'The demand for change ... does not arise out of the *impossibility* of tolerating the existing state of affairs, but out of the *possibility* of no longer having to tolerate it'.[51]

Gorz realises that autonomous self-organised actions at the local level – for example, factory, community, university – do not necessarily lead to the development of socialism. Struggles for workers' power at the factory level, for example, must spread to the company level, and then on to a wider industrial level. The same is true of citizens' struggles. Unless the struggle spreads (outward and forward) gains in autonomy can easily be lost. To prevent this from happening it is necessary to protect one's gains, and this means that the struggle must continue. Its continuity is essential to its spreading. So, too, is the co-ordination of struggles. The need for some means of synthesising, both ideologically and practically, the range of local struggles and diverse (albeit anti-capitalist) demands calls for organisation. Gorz entrusts this task to 'the party'.

The co-ordination and ideological synthesis of struggles cannot be conducted by those who are not part of the struggle. Ideally the party must be built up 'from within' self-organised actions and movements and 'not from without as their external leadership'. In other words,

> the party is to be the means of the working class's own conquest
> of power and not a new machine for exercising power on *behalf*
> of the working class. Without a revolutionary party that stimulates
> effective self-expression from below and offers a unifying political
> perspective to autonomous and 'spontaneous' struggles, there
> can be no lasting revolutionary movement; conversely, without
> a movement that draws its vitality from the imagination and
> inventiveness of the masses, the party ... is doomed to become
> a force of repression and domination and to waste its energies
> in internecine struggles and conspirational tactics.[52]

All of this presupposes that the party has its 'finger on the pulse'
in a theoretically informed way. Armed with a critique of capitalism,
and with a vision of a socialist future, the party is in a position both
to co-ordinate struggles and to identify new sites of struggle around
demands reflecting the needs and aspirations of workers and
citizens. In this regard the leadership role of the party exists in order to

> express the permanent nature of the struggle and its objectives,
> even in periods of reflux. It foreshadows the workers' state and
> demonstrates to the working class its ability to become the
> ruling class. It embodies the presence of socialism under
> capitalism ... it ensures the survival of the movement, and of
> revolutionary consciousness, during fallow periods when the
> balance of forces rules out decisive action.[53]

But 'to fulfil these tasks', Gorz maintains, 'the party must appear
both as a memory and as the prefiguration of struggles more
advanced than those which are possible at any given moment'.[54]

Capitalism, as Gorz persistently shows, is full of contradictions
– production for profit rather than need underpins contradictions
in the 'simple' reproduction of labour power (the satisfaction of
basic needs) and in the 'wider' reproduction of labour power (the
subordination of creativity and autonomy in production for profit);
in contradictions between the short- and-long term interests of
capitalism; in forcing individuals to subsidise the collective needs
(for example, roads) of capital while failing to provide for people's
collective needs other than by the provision of goods for individual
purchase; and in getting individuals to suffer and pay for the social
costs of the pursuit of profit (for example, pollution). One of the
main tasks of the party is to expose these contradictions, not in
abstract terms, but in terms relevant to the experience of workers
and citizens, in order to stimulate actions that can ultimately
destroy capitalism from within.

The agitational role of the party, however, will be ineffective, and
even counterproductive, unless it is rooted in the experience of mass
struggle, and unless the party conducts itself in a thoroughly

democratic way. As we have noted, ideally the party, that is the 'leadership' group, emerges from those engaged in mass struggles. But this may not happen. In such an event Gorz recognises a need for an 'initial vanguard group', made up of 'students and people with some political education'. But the function of this external vanguard is to act as a catalyst for an internal vanguard. The external vanguard is thus a temporary group. In his consideration of vanguard groups in building a revolutionary party, Gorz is particularly sensitive to the dangers of self-appointed vanguards pursuing a direction that could lead to the party becoming an authoritarian, centralised, bureaucratic organisation. Since one of the tasks of the revolutionary party, its most spectacular one, is that of transferring state power to the people, it is essential that the party reflects this permanently in its

> life style and way of exercising leadership. The party must be above all a centre of permanent debate and direct democracy; it must encourage collective self-determination and self-rule everywhere; it must not be a mere organisation specialising in politics and political leadership, but also a place where people come together to experience a different life, to work out practically and theoretically the politics of life. The meanings of 'politics' and 'party' must themselves be subverted. They must be seen as being nothing but the conscious collective practice of liberation.[55]

Much of Gorz's thinking on the role of the revolutionary party had been formed prior to the spontaneous revolts of 1968. Gorz had anticipated these revolts. 'It is in education that industrial capitalism will provoke the revolts which it attempts to avoid in its factories.'[56] The main reason why Gorz was able to make this accurate prediction is that he knows enough about the experience of autonomy to know that it is self-generating. Thus 'once a certain level of culture has been reached, the need for autonomy, the need to develop one's abilities freely and to give a purpose to one's life is experienced with the same intensity as an unsatisfied physiological necessity'.[57] He knew, too, that this need was experienced by workers – hence the emphasis of his strategy on autonomy. But he also knew that if workers' demands were to generate the momentum necessary to deliver socialism then it was absolutely necessary that a revolutionary party capable of organising struggles should develop. No such party developed.

The division of labour

The events of 1968 occasioned a variety of responses among left-wing intellectuals. Many were plunged into despair which, in some, took the form of withdrawing from any intellectual engagement with politics. In contrast, Gorz felt that there were important lessons to be learned for the struggle for socialism. This was made clear in the post-1968 Introduction of the English edition of *Socialism and Revolution*. For Gorz the struggle had to continue. And this meant that the attack on alienation had to continue, which, in turn, propelled Gorz toward a stronger critique of the labour process, and in particular, of the division of labour under capitalism.

In *Strategy for Labour* Gorz had referred to 'techniques of domination founded on ... the organisation of work'.[58] In *Socialism and Revolution* Gorz had more to say on this front: capitalism, 'by methods of division of labour which, often without technical necessity, are methods of domination, sets out to produce decomposed, molecularised, humiliated men, whom it can then dominate in society'.[59] The division of labour, Gorz went on to demonstrate in a number of essays, was, under capitalism, primarily a means of *domination*.[60] Rather than the division of labour being seen as a 'neutral' necessity for efficient production, reflecting the 'neutrality' of science and technology, Gorz argues that it is far from neutral. The class domination inherent in the capitalist division of labour is illustrated by 'a vicious circle' at the heart of the labour process;

1) since the purpose of production is not the satisfaction of the producers' needs, but the extortion of surplus labour, capitalist production cannot rely upon the workers' willingness to work;
2) the less capitalist management wishes to rely upon the willingness of the workers to work, the more extraneous, regimented and idiotic work has to become;
3) the more extraneous, regimented and idiotic work becomes the less capitalist management can rely upon the workers' willingness.[61]

Gorz concludes from this that

> because relations at the workplace are established right from the word go on the basis of antagonistic class relations, hierarchical work organisation and control always appear to capital to be the necessary preconditions for production *and an end in themselves*. They are built into the very methods and tools used in production and they appear to be technical necessities of the production process itself.[62]

This analysis holds a number of implications for Gorz's strategy for the struggle for socialism. It reinforces his argument that the traditional communist movement's route to socialism is a non-starter. The movement's belief that the forces of production developed under capitalism could serve a future socialist society was unfounded. As

Gorz puts it: 'There is no such thing as communism without a communist life-style or "culture"; but a communist life-style cannot be based on the technology, institutions and division of labour which derive from capitalism.'[63]

Gorz's sensitivity to the impact of 'forced labour' imposed on manual workers, and his assessment of the 'functionaries' (technical and supervisory workers) of class domination, distanced him from the view (which he had briefly courted) that the 'leaders' of workers' struggles for socialism would come from skilled, technical and scientific workers. The basis of this view was that the creative autonomy embodied in 'intellectual' workers would be so frustrated by the constraints of production for profit, in addition to the realisation by these workers of their pivotal role in production, that they would be at the forefront of struggles for more autonomy in the workplace. However, this 'pivotal' role is not restricted to the value of their labour power for profit. It is just as much a political and ideological role in so far as these workers occupy a position in the hierarchical division of labour which places them in a superior, supervisory position in relation to those performing low-skilled tasks.

> *Technically*, the factory could dispense with such functionaries but their *political* function is to perpetuate the workers' dependence, subordination and separation from the means and process of production. By making control a separate function, the factory hierarchy is instrumental in denying the workers any possible control over the conditions and methods of machine production. Only in this way can the means and process of production be set up as an alien, autonomous power that exacts the workers' submission.[64]

In his observations on the revolts of 1968, Gorz noted that 'technical, scientific and managerial employees ... were not (except in individual cases) prepared to question ideologically the overall rationality of the capitalist division of labour'.[65] Later Gorz argues that 'their struggle against hierarchy and authority is usually part and parcel of their demand for the reinstatement of the privileges they once enjoyed as members of the professional "middle class"'.[66] This, of course, is hardly the attitude of those likely to lead the revolution. In contrast, Gorz observed that 'the demands of young manual workers tended to be more radical'.[67] They sought full control of production and the elimination of hierarchy and state power. Gorz suggests that:

> The driving motive behind these demands was the feeling that the monotony of the work, its harassing speed, its minute specialisation and fragmentation, the systems of job evaluation and wage differentiation were not functional to the process of

production as such, but were arbitrary and despotic devices to keep workers in subjection, and to destroy the initiative, inventiveness, autonomy, creativeness and skill that – however unskilled the job – they realised they possessed.[68]

Gorz, in full empathy with the demands of young manual workers, continued to advocate workers' control into the 1970s. At the same time he was continually monitoring the impact of technological developments on the skill requirements of production, and identifying contradictions in the capitalist system that could be exploited in the struggle for socialism. Given the level of technological development, and rate of technological innovation, at the time, Gorz could see the futility of training specialists. Many technical skills were obsolete within five years. Yet industrial capitalists preferred specialists to the multi-skilled, flexible worker who was more adaptable to changes in production technology. The specialist was cheaper and easier to *control*. The latter was promoted by their training for subservience to industrial controllers. Gorz was particularly astute at exposing such contradictions, not only for their impact on the experience of work, but also for their impact on the education system. In his identification of a rebellious attitude amongst those 'educated' for subordination, Gorz touched upon an attitude that was to spread, and find theoretical expression in his later work.

> Why should they put up with the disciplinarian and authoritarian methods of training when this training cannot either enable them to rise socially or get them work that is interesting and helps them to develop their faculties? If success at school does you no good, well fuck the schools and fuck the system. You might as well decide for yourself what to do and what to learn.[69]

Before long such an attitude was to harden and incorporate more sober dimensions among an increasing number of people. Production technology, particularly in its use of micro-electronics, began to transform the nature of work and the total labour requirements of the advanced societies. Automation was not only eliminating jobs at an unprecedented rate, it was de-skilling them too, often to the point of absurdity. The workplace, especially in the productive sector, was no longer the centre for decision-making with regards to production policy. It was more the product of decisions made elsewhere – often abroad. Full-blown workers' control was no longer feasible. Gorz had to rethink his strategy for socialism. As we shall see he has been able to do just this without compromising the critique of capitalism which he developed in his early work.

Gorzian Themes

It is not unusual for *Farewell to the Working Class* to be seen as a text that represents a radical break in Gorz's thinking – an abandonment of Gorz's commitment to class politics. One commentator even suggests that *Critique of Economic Reason*, published some eight years later, demonstrates a further, radical evolution in Gorz's thinking from that of 1980.[1] There have been a few shifts in focus in Gorz's thinking. Indeed, it would be most surprising if this was not the case, given that Gorz's writings span almost half a century. As Marcuse argued:

> Not to confront the Marxian concepts with the development of capitalism and not to draw the consequences from this confrontation for the political practice leads to a mechanistic repetition of a 'basic vocabulary', a petrification of Marxian theory into a rhetoric with hardly any relation to reality ... A theory which has not caught up with the practice of capitalism cannot possibly guide the practice aiming at the abolition of capitalism.[2]

There is no doubt at all that Gorz's thinking has kept up with developments in capitalism. But, just as in the 1960s, Gorz has addressed these developments from a secure foundation of a commitment to an emancipatory socialist project. We would prefer to see this commitment as underpinning his political writings and in giving them a very clear sense of continuity. The shifts in focus in Gorz's thinking need to be understood within the context of his underlying commitment to emancipation.

It is a relatively simple matter to provide an abundance of textual support for our insistence on the underlying coherence of Gorz's project. For example, it can be noted that in 1991 Gorz maintains that:

> A political strategy centred on the reduction of working hours may be the main lever with which we can shift the balance within society, and put an end to the domination of the political sphere by the economic. And this would mean the extinction of capitalism.[3]

This statement is representative of Gorz's advocacy of a politics of time, arguably the basis of his notoriety. It was first given detailed expression in *Farewell to the Working Class,* and is often cited as the main reason why this text is said to break radically from Gorz's earlier positions. While it is true that the politics of time has become the centrepiece of Gorz's political strategy, the claim that this represents a radical change in his thinking cannot be supported. As early as *Strategy for Labour* Gorz approvingly quotes Marcuse: 'economic freedom would mean freedom *from* the economy – from being controlled by economic forces and relationships; from the daily struggle for existence, from earning a living'.[4] In the next paragraph he argues that:

> The only humanism which can succeed the humanism of work is the humanism of free activity and of self-management at all levels. It presupposes that individuals instead of seeing themselves and being seen as means of society and of production, be seen and see themselves as ends, that no longer the time at work, but free time becomes the standard of wealth.[5]

Our main task in this chapter, however, is not that of establishing the continuities in Gorz's thinking, but rather to focus on Gorz's later writings; that is from *Ecology as Politics* onwards. We merely want to alert the reader to the fact that Gorz's later writings are continuous with, and a development of, his earlier work. It is within this development that we encounter shifts in emphasis. Needless to say, an engagement with Gorz's earlier work does provide a fuller understanding of his more recent thought.

A number of themes interweave throughout Gorz's thinking. Since *Ecology as Politics* ecological concerns constitute an important theme that is closely bound up with Gorz's critique of capitalism, his vision of a future socialism, his hope for an emancipatory use of the latest technologies, his advocacy of a politics of time and how this may radically change our patterns of consumption. Similarly, Gorz's analysis and critique of work is not only steeped in his continuing concern with alienation and how it is maintained by the division of labour imposed by the use of high-tech production, it is, at the same time, informed by his demonstration that inflated working hours are compatible with the logic of capitalism – the pursuit of profit in the consumption of unnecessary goods. More than this, his analysis of work is conducted with emancipatory goals in mind by spelling out the limits to autonomy within work and the possibilities for the expansion of a sphere of autonomy via a policy of reduced working hours. Thus Gorz's analysis and critique of work does not so much touch upon, but is rather penetrated by, his critique of capitalism, his understanding of how needs are manipulated, the repercussions of affluent consumption for ecological balance, and the value of a politics of time for delivering an emancipatory socialism.

In this chapter we shall concentrate on the themes that have been most prominent in Gorz's more recent work. As we have shown above, these themes are closely interwoven. For clarity of presentation, however, it will be necessary to disentangle the themes into the following: freedom/alienation; autonomy/heteronomy; work; needs and consumerism; technology and political ecology; capitalism/socialism; the politics of time.

The question can be raised as to whether or not some themes are more important than others. The manner in which the themes interpenetrate each other suggests not. However, there is a sense in which the freedom/alienation theme is the most fundamental one in so far as it provides the existential basis of Gorzian thought, which is rooted in lived experience. It thus makes sense to start with our everyday experience.

Freedom/alienation

We are born into a social world in which we are dependent on others for our survival and wellbeing. From birth we are subject to the forces of socialisation. This is inescapable. And it is our early socialisation which initially obliges us to become a self that is not our own – even if we were left to our own devices. Of course, the latter is impossible. As Gorz puts it, 'Socialisation prevents us from belonging entirely to ourselves, but we would not have belonged to ourselves if it had been different or even – though this is impossible – if there had been no socialisation at all.'[6] Whatever the social being we are obliged to become through socialisation it never entirely coincides 'with our innermost experience'.[7] Thus 'childhood is an original condition of alienation'.[8] Our experience of alienation is 'the social negation of each individual's experience of freedom'.[9] Thus our experience of alienation is the precondition for our freedom. In the Sartrian sense we are 'condemned to be free'.

We are both alienated and free. No matter how restricting the social circumstances we nevertheless retain our freedom – it is part and parcel of what we are. There is no point arguing about this, it is a fact of existence. As Gorz says, it 'is not a thesis … but an insight'.[10] Nevertheless Gorz recognises that the extent to which we can use and develop our freedom will vary according to the social circumstances confronting us. While he maintains that 'the individual experiences his or her being as always free, in all circumstances',[11] the expression of this freedom may be severely restricted. Gorz offers the example of prisoners to illustrate the repressive character of alienation and their use of their freedom. Prisoners are not and cannot be what they have been sentenced to be, and the impossibility of accepting, of getting used to this sentence constitutes their feeling of freedom, which may be frustrated or negated, but persists as negation of what negates it, even if it cannot express itself in a positive way. People will repeatedly rise up against – even rebel against – the severest repression, even when the situation appears hopeless.[12]

Gorz goes on to state that 'prisoners experience and assert their freedom by covertly building relations with fellow prisoners and constantly preparing their escape or making plans about what they will do when they are released'.[13] Of course the *experience* of imprisonment, of being a prisoner, is not confined to that small minority who are locked up behind bars. Some women, for example, refer to their marriages or home as 'a prison'. From time to time children make similar references to their experience of their families and schools. And it is not unusual for people in all sorts of jobs to experience their employment as a form of imprisonment. Some of this experience can be attributed to 'the non-coincidence of the individual subject with the "identity" which society obliges him – or gives him the means – to express'.[14] But it is precisely this, Gorz tells us, which is 'at the root of both individual autonomy and all cultural creation'.[15]

Yet some individuals do become more autonomous than others. The main reason for this, Gorz argues, is to be found in the variation within socialisation practices. Socialisation is essentially a process whereby the individual is manipulated and taught to become a 'normal' adult capable of fitting with society. But initial socialisation within the family is far from uniform. 'The more contradictory the family background, the more it becomes impossible to follow its values, or even to see any values to follow – and so the more the child is forced to be autonomous.'[16] It could be said that this is descriptive of 'parental neglect'. No doubt some individuals develop their autonomy in response to neglect, but for Gorz the achievement of autonomy is better served by parental support. This is especially important if 'the non-socialised part' of individuals' lives is to prevail 'over the socialised part'.[17]

Parental support for the child's autonomy can help to maintain the child's sense of himself or herself as autonomous in the face of the self-alienating pressures of schooling. Schools, as institutions serving their parent society, enact practices that do very little to enhance the development of autonomy. In fact, Gorz argues that schooling is involved in the 'destruction of autonomous capacities'.[18] It does this primarily by involving the child in prescribed activities determined by others. The only spaces available for the child's own self-determination, the child's own independence and creativity, fall *within* the wider determinations imposed by the school. For much of the time controlled by schooling, the child will be obliged to follow the rules and submit himself or herself to the authority of others. In other words the child will be coerced into subordinating her or his own autonomy to the authority of the school. This is how schools prepare children for a future within the capitalist division of labour – a future in which work is divorced from any notion of 'producing for oneself', and which, like schooling, is predetermined. It is a future, too, in which

> having been deprived of all possibility of control over the purpose or the character of labour, the realm of freedom becomes exclusively that of non-work periods. But since all creative or productive activity *of any social consequence* is nevertheless denied during 'free' time, this freedom is itself reduced to a choice amongst objects of consumption and passive distractions.[19]

It is clear that capitalist society does not need autonomous individuals, the more so as it spreads its domination over civil society. Here 'relations of cooperation and mutual aid', and the 'totality of exchanges and communications' which 'once constituted the "life" of the neighbourhood or small town' have been replaced 'by the purchase of institutionally produced goods and services'.[20] Civil society was once constituted of activities that individuals performed for themselves and each other, that is, activities drawing on individual and collective autonomy. This is why Gorz identifies the decline of civil society as another source of the destruction of autonomous capacities.

The onslaught against autonomy conducted by schooling makes perfect sense if human beings are to become cogs in a machine, automatons who are functionally integrated into the social system.

> Schooling discourages independence and versatility in favour of graded 'qualifications', which have the essential characteristic of having no use value for the person who acquires them, but only an exchange value in the marketplace. You can't do anything for yourself with what you learn in school. The only way to make use of the qualifications bestowed by schools is through the mediation of a third person, by trying to sell oneself on the 'job market'.[21]

When there was some order to the job market, when the individual's position in the job market bore some relation to graded qualifications, the denial of autonomy was, for the most part, rewarded by relatively secure employment and the wage packet that went with it. Today, however, this is no longer the case. There is no clear link between scholastic achievement and future employment. Besides, most forms of employment have become both insecure and meaningless. Consequently fewer people are able to identify with their jobs and fewer people make work the central focus of their lives. Early socialisation is followed by an uncertain future.

> Socialisation no longer guarantees individuals a *place* in a 'social order', no longer ensures a sense of belonging and an 'identity'. Each person occupies multiple functions, roles and places without being able to identify with any one of them; in consequence, everyone has to construct an identity for him- or herself.[22]

All of this may well suit the continuing dominance of the capitalist system. There is, after all, money to be made from the commodification of identities and all the various facets of the identity industry. The problem here, however, is that individuals are seeking *fulfilling* and *meaningful* identities, and these cannot be bought. They can only be achieved and lived by individuals exercising autonomy. Thus Gorz tells us that the

> choice of autonomy of 'self-realisation', is in fact the only response by which the subject can face up to the way society has disintegrated into a multiplicity of specialised, technicized systems, each addressing a partial aspect of social reality and everyday life with no coherence between them.[23]

The obvious question to ask is: how can individuals, whose autonomous capacities have been seriously underdeveloped, possibly make this 'choice of autonomy'? In many respects the answer to this question will unfold throughout this chapter. Everything that Gorz has written is dedicated, directly or indirectly, to identifying the obstacles to individual freedom and *what can be done* to create the social conditions which best serve the individual's choice of autonomy.

But, some critics might ask: is not Gorz's mission inherently doomed to failure? Is it not the case that Gorz has argued himself into a corner out of which he cannot escape? He seems to posit an all-powerful society working against individuals' capacities to positively realise their freedom; yet ultimately he still champions the freedom of the individual. Is this credible? If Gorz can show us how we can become more autonomous, is he not providing a recipe for further social disintegration? In short how can there be a society of autonomous individuals?

Gorz is fully aware of these kinds of questions and their various sources. He has made his position quite clear. Gorz's vision is not that of isolated individuals doing their own thing with no regard for others. For Gorz autonomous action always involves the individual taking responsibility for her or his actions. But, more than this, to choose freedom implies wanting or desiring one's own freedom. In other words to choose freedom is not a light or random matter – it is an intentional, conscious act. Gorz is not advocating the freedom of some to the detriment of others – freedom is a universal value. The conscious choice of freedom thus also implies recognition of the freedom of others.

> It is impossible to *want* one's own freedom without recognising other people's, and wanting to be recognised by them as free, as the originator of one's actions and creations. Reciprocity is always the reciprocal recognition of the freedom of others, not merely toleration.[24]

Gorz's concept of freedom is inherently social, but not entirely so – there are areas of existence, like love for example, which, Gorz maintains, are and should be asocial. Social freedom involves voluntary co-operation. As Gorz argues, 'In order to become the subject of my actions, I must change the world, but I can only do this in co-operation with all the others.' 'But,' he goes on to warn, 'there are dozens of forms of co-operation in which individuals are needed only as tools, as obedient soldiers'. So, while significant gains in social freedom can only come about collectively, these gains will be meaningless (and may even become alienating and oppressive) unless they are also experienced as gains in individual freedom. 'If one begins with the collective, then the individual is generally lost forever.'[25]

Gorz is adamant that 'the choice of freedom is the only possible morality. There can be no other.'[26] But, 'if conscience is not the determining instance of what I can or must do or be, then morality becomes a function of the requirements of the social order, and everyone is required to be and do what society needs'.[27] For Gorz the relationship and balance between social requirements on the one hand, and individual and social freedom on the other, is of crucial importance. It is to this that we now turn.

Autonomy/heteronomy

Following Marx, Gorz identifies the root of alienation in the capitalist division of labour. The latter 'separates consumption and production'.

> Since no one is the subject of their productive work any longer, they cannot be the subject of their consumption either. Because we do not produce what we use and do not use what we produce, in neither working nor consuming are we 'at home', as Marx put it, are we 'ourselves'.[28]

Instead of individuals voluntarily co-operating with others to produce, as co-producers for their self-determined needs, we, as workers, are compelled to operate in a system of production designed for profit rather than need. This system determines our actions as workers. In other words, 'all work performed within social production is necessarily heteronomous'.[29] Gorz elaborates:

> Whatever level of skill is required, its form and content are determined by technical imperatives independent of all individual choice and interpretation; these imperatives severely limit the scope for individual judgment and initiative. This does not mean that heteronomy necessarily implies oppression and domination, boredom and/or exploitation. But it does necessarily imply the absence of individual control over the kinds of skill required and the overall purpose of collective work, and thus a degree of alienation.[30]

Gorz does not deny that some autonomy within heteronomous work is possible, but he insists that it is a limited, trivial form of autonomy within hetero-regulation. As he says, 'Work is no longer the worker's own activity.'[31] Work, rather 'belongs to the machinery of social production, is allocated and programmed by it, remaining external to the individuals upon whom it is imposed'.[32]

The sphere of heteronomy is not confined to productive work. The system of production requires an elaborate infrastructure involving, for example, the development of communications, transport systems, state administration and services, which not only generates work, but also imposes itself upon us in the form of the regulation of our conduct. Thus:

> As a structured system, society is necessarily external to its members. It is not the product of free voluntary co-operation. Individuals do not produce it by starting from themselves: they produce it on the ground of its own inert exigencies, adapting themselves to the jobs, functions, skills, environments and hierarchical relations pre-established by society to assure its cohesive functioning.[33]

Not surprisingly a major consequence of hetero-determination is that individuals increasingly experience a split between working and living. The latter is increasingly confined to the private sphere. People find that 'their professional and private lives are dominated by norms and values that are radically different from one another, if not indeed contradictory'. The split between professional and private life, between working and living, between hetero-determination and self-determination, 'produces a split within the lives of individuals themselves'. Gorz continues:

> Within large organisations, professional success requires a will to succeed according to the purely technical efficiency criteria

of the functions one occupies, irrespective of content. It demands a spirit of competition and opportunism, combined with subservience towards superiors. This will be recompensed and *compensated* – in the private sphere by a comfortable, opulent, hedonistic lifestyle.[34]

What Gorz is getting at here is that 'professional success becomes the *means* of achieving private comfort and pleasures that have no relation with the qualities demanded by professional life'. He goes on to point out that 'these qualities are not connected with personal virtue, and private life is sheltered from the imperatives of professional life'.[35] Of course as professional life has become more competitive, demands on the individual increase, and, as a consequence the private sphere shrinks to little more than instantaneous consumption. Drawing on Weber, Gorz argues that the 'weight of bureaucracy has indeed increased, programmed hetero-regulation has become more and more dehumanising, and the "shell of bondage" has become *at the same time increasingly constraining and increasingly comfortable*'.[36]

While very few are professionally successful, it would be wrong to assume that it is only this minority that live a life that is largely hetero-determined. In times of high unemployment many, arguably most, workers feel obliged to adopt the behaviour of the successful, not to gain success, but merely to hang on to their jobs. Whether or not 'playing the game' brings with it compensatory comforts is largely a matter of luck.

We seem to have moved a long way from Gorz's insight that we are all free. But have we? It is precisely because Gorz 'knows' that we are free in an ontological sense that he is compelled to point out the extent to which society obliges us to behave in unfree ways. Gorz also knows that this does not have to be so. There are alternatives. In preparing the ground for these alternatives, or at least the one most favoured by Gorz, it will be useful to consider the relation between what Marx called the 'realm of necessity' and Gorz's (following Illich)[37] realm or sphere of heteronomy.

'In essence,' Gorz states, 'what is necessary is what we need as social individuals to live in the socio-cultural context of our own civilisation.'[38] The realm of necessity in Marx's lifetime involved both 'work for economic ends and work-for-oneself in the domestic sphere' serving 'essentially to produce what was necessary and allowed practically no time for anything else'.[39] Gorz argues that today, in contrast, the realm of necessity has been industrialised to such an extent (including labour-saving devices in the domestic sphere) that

we are therefore less in thrall to the 'necessities' of existence than to the external determination of our lives and our activity by the imperatives of a social apparatus of production and organisation which provides willy-nilly both *the essential and the superfluous, the economic and the anti-economic, the productive and destructive.*[40]

Thus while the vast majority of us are all dependent, directly or indirectly, on employment to satisfy our needs (the necessary), what we must do in employment involves us in producing both the necessary and the non-necessary. Gorz maintains that

this is why, in our daily experience, it is no longer so much the freedom/necessity distinction which is decisive, but the autonomy/heteronomy opposition. Freedom consists less (or rather consists less and less) in freeing ourselves from the work we need to do to live and more in freeing ourselves from heteronomy, that is, in reconquering spaces of autonomy in which we can *will what we are doing and take responsibility for it.*[41]

As we shall see throughout this chapter, the distinction between the sphere of heteronomy and the sphere of autonomy plays a crucial role in Gorz's social critique, especially his critique of most forms of work, and in his politics. But from the discussion this far it might be assumed that Gorz equates the sphere of autonomy with the private sphere. This is misleading. He acknowledges that under the dominance of the sphere of heteronomy the private sphere is for most people the only sphere in which they can exercise meaningful autonomy. Furthermore, it needs to be emphasised that for Gorz neither autonomous activities nor the sphere of autonomy bear any relation to the widely celebrated 'consumer autonomy'. Gorz is referring to something far more substantial. The sphere of autonomy or of 'individual sovereignty is not based on a mere desire to consume, nor solely upon relaxation and leisure activities'. Rather,

It is based, more profoundly, upon activities unrelated to any economic goal which are an end in themselves; communication, giving, creating and aesthetic enjoyment, the production and reproduction of life, tenderness, the realisation of physical, sensuous and intellectual capacities, the creation of non-commodity use-values (shared goods or services) that could not be produced as commodities because of their unprofitability – in short, the whole range of activities that make up the fabric of existence and therefore occupy a primordial rather than a subordinate place.[42]

It is one of Gorz's major tasks to spell out how the sphere of autonomy can be expanded to 'occupy a primordial rather than subordinate place' in society. In pursuing this task Gorz develops a strategy for the labour movement which departs from the revolutionary Marxist orthodoxy that Gorz represented, albeit in humanistic form, in *Strategy for Labour* and *Socialism and Revolution*. Gorz argues that 'the political imperatives of the class struggle have ... prevented the labour movement from examining the desire for autonomy as a *specifically existential demand*'. Gorz continues:

> The fact that this demand might be politically embarrassing has no bearing at all upon its irreducible reality. Needs may exist for other than political reasons and continue to exist in spite of countervailing political imperatives. This is true of certain existential needs (of an aesthetic, erotic, cultural or emotional sort) and is most particularly true of the need for autonomy.[43]

Gorz's strategy for the expansion of the sphere of autonomy implies a rejection of 'the traditional strategy and organisational forms of the working-class movement'. As Gorz says, 'It is no longer a question of winning power as a worker, but of winning the power no longer to function as a worker.'[44] We shall see that Gorz does not mean by this that work can be abolished. Far from it. But he does see a tremendous opportunity to reduce the sphere of heteronomous work as the basis for an expanded sphere of autonomy.

Work

Gorz has written extensively on work. All we wish to do here is to illustrate how his analysis and critique of work is driven by, and contributes to, his emancipatory project. For Gorz there are two forms of work: heteronomous work, that is 'work for economic ends', and 'domestic labour and work-for-oneself'. Beyond work there is autonomous activity. We have already seen that heteronomous work is inevitably alienating. Yet 'if it wasn't for the sphere of social production with its division of labour and relatively large and complex production units we would have to work a great deal more to produce the bare necessities'.[45] This is of the utmost importance to Gorz. The very efficiency of the division of labour generated by the productive forces, which makes work alienating, actually reduces the need for work for economic ends.

> The division of labour and knowledge into fragmented but complementary technical skills is the only means by which it is possible to accumulate and put to work the huge stocks of knowledge embodied in machines, industrial systems and processes of every scale and dimension.[46]

It is thus undesirable to abolish this division of labour. Gorz provides three basic reasons why a 'sector of socialised production is ... indispensable'.

First, only the socialisation of knowledge, and of its storage and transmission, allows a plentiful supply of technologically advanced tools.

Second, the highly productive machinery capable of turning out such tools at low cost (whether they be cathode tubes or ball-bearings) is beyond the means of local communities or towns.

Third, if the time spent on heteronomous labour is to be reduced to a minimum, then everyone will have to do some work.[47]

So, against the battle cries of trade unionists who bemoan the loss of jobs as a result of automation, Gorz's strategy accommodates the reduction of labour. But as we shall see later, it is a strategy which also eliminates unemployment. For the moment, however, there are two further points to consider in Gorz's argument for a retention of a sphere of socialised production.

First, with increasing automation socialised production can become even more efficient, that is, less demanding of energy and labour time. And if the productive forces are restricted to the production for need (rather than profit) then even less energy and labour time will be required by them. It will thus be possible to shrink the sphere in which we work for economic ends, thereby potentially increasing the spaces of autonomy available for the individual. In relation to our earlier discussion, alienated labour is not to be reduced by workers taking control of the means of production (whatever this might mean), but by a reduction of time devoted to working in the sphere of heteronomy. Of course, for this to happen 'everyone will have to do some work'. This brings us to the second point.

Gorz, in his analysis of the changing nature of work, has been one of those who has commented at length on the fact that by comparison with pre-industrial and non-industrial forms of work, most socialised production today involves workers in de-skilled work. Indeed the de-skilled nature of what most workers have to do to earn a living is a major source of meaninglessness. De-skilled work is an insult to human intelligence and does not begin to tap the range of capacities and skills embodied in individual workers. But, for Gorz's emancipatory project this has its advantages.

Everyone can only work efficiently in the sector of heteronomous production if the complex knowledge required for the efficient execution of their tasks is embodied in industrial processes stored in sophisticated machinery, so that the (social) skills needed for each activity can be acquired in a short period of time. Only standardised simplification allows the mass of socially necessary labour to be distributed among the population as a whole in such a way that the average working day is reduced to a few hours.[48]

The advantage of 'standardised simplification', that is de-skilled work that anyone can do, means that if everyone is to work the nature of the work itself is no obstacle to such a policy. Even so, Gorz recognises that not all work in socialised production is de-skilled. With the introduction of computerisation there has emerged the need for multi-skilled process workers, often working in relatively autonomous groups. Computerisation imposes its own standardisations such that the kind of work done, irrespective of its location (brewery or nuclear power station), is essentially the same – monitoring and controlling the production process at a distance, that is, via display screens. This kind of work is transferable across locations, giving the process worker considerable mobility compared with those specialised in highly specific and narrow tasks. With very little training, Gorz argues, the skills of the multi-skilled process worker can 'be *rendered commonplace*'. By this he means 'that the work they do' will not 'become de-skilled and monotonous, but that *a much greater number of people will be able to acquire the skills it entails*'.[49]

This may not please those groups who wish to maintain their elite status – but then, Gorz has no time for elites and the inequalities that go with them. The most important point to be made about automated socialised production is that it saves labour time, but in a capitalist system these 'savings' are used up in unnecessary production, and what cannot be thus used fetches up in unemployment, casual, temporary and part-time employment. In other words, social inequalities are exacerbated. And, as if to further humiliate those who are involuntarily marginalised, the capitalist system offers them jobs as servants, that is, work in some form of commodified personal service. Gorz observes that personal services is the biggest growth area in the economy. Advocates of 'tertiarisation' or 'new employment-richer growth', the names economists give to the development of a 'service society', often speak of the limitless employment opportunities that can be exploited by transforming 'into acts of paid service those activities which people have hitherto performed for themselves'.[50]

Gorz has two main objections to this development. First, it heightens social inequality. What enables the development of a growing service sector is the 'dualisation of society' – a society split in two, those in stable, well-paid jobs, and the rest: the unemployed and those with insecure and low-paid employment. The well-paid are in a position to purchase personal services. But as Gorz says, 'To buy someone else's time to increase your own leisure or comfort is merely to purchase the work of a servant.' Even when the purchaser and the servant are of the same economic status,

> *you are claiming the privilege of unloading your chores on to someone else*; you are implicitly asserting that there must be people to take on your chores, *people who are fit only to do what you find boring or repugnant* – in short, people whose vocation is to serve. In a word, inferiors.[51]

Gorz's second major objection is focused on the consequences of the development of personal services for the private sphere, and for autonomous activities.

> By dint of monetizing, professionalising and transforming into jobs the few remaining production and service activities we still perform for ourselves, might we not reduce our capacity to look after ourselves almost to the point where it disappears, thus undermining the foundations of existential autonomy, not to mention the foundations of lived sociality and the fabric of human relationships?[52]

To grasp the full significance of what Gorz is saying here it is necessary to enter into the heart of his precise conception of work. The various activities we perform, Gorz argues, do not obey the same rationality. Autonomous activities are 'those activities which are themselves their own end'.

> They are valued for and in themselves not because they have no other objective than the satisfaction and pleasure they procure, but because *the action which achieves the goal is as much a source of satisfaction as the achievement of the goal itself*: the end is reflected in the means and vice versa.[53]

Autonomous activities are those activities in which 'subjects experience their own sovereignty and fulfil themselves as persons'.[54] Clearly, as Gorz says, 'Commodity activities are ... excluded by their very essence from this category.'[55] The primary purpose of commodity activities is economic. Obviously people may receive payment for autonomous activities, but as soon as monetary considerations determine what one does, the activity in question is no longer autonomous; it is no longer 'an unconditional giving of oneself'. We, well most of us, 'know' this to be the case.

> This gift ... [of oneself] ... is recognised precisely in its *incommensurable* value when the public 'honours' it by a payment which never has the sense of a purchase, that is, as giving an equivalent amount in exchange: an audience shows its appreciation of an artist by standing ovations even when it has paid dearly for the opportunity to hear her or him.[56]

Additionally, autonomous activities are freely determined activities reflecting conscious choices, and as such they are free of necessity. It should be clear that autonomous activities are not, as some may think, self-indulgent and socially isolated activities. In embracing the notion of 'an unconditional giving of oneself' autonomous activities can be inherently social. It is, for example, this very unconditional giving of oneself, Gorz argues, which is the essence of genuine caring. Thus Gorz maintains that in a society in which time is no longer scarce, many caring and teaching activities are best done by volunteers. This does not mean that doctors, for example, should not be paid, but rather that monetary reward is an inappropriate and irrelevant motivation in the case of genuine care.

When time is no longer scarce the sphere of private sovereignty in which we carry out work-for-ourselves, currently reduced in the main to self-maintenance and chores, can be reclaimed from the clutches of state provided or commercial services. What characterises work-for-oneself (and why it is called 'work') is the *necessity* of it, and that the person performing it is the sole beneficiary and/or serves the needs of others in the domestic unit. While it is the necessity of domestic labour that distinguishes it from autonomous activities, this does not mean that it cannot be 'voluntary' work. Indeed, Gorz argues that the private sphere can be an arena of convivial relations, 'so long as I participate in its development, its organisation and its maintenance in voluntary co-operation with other users'. He goes on to point out that:

> Work 'for oneself' then finds its natural extension in work 'for ourselves', just as the community of the family finds an extension in the informal co-operative that provides immediate services and in the informal associations of mutual aid between neighbours.[57]

Importantly, Gorz insists that 'commodity relations cannot exist between members of a family or a community – or that community will be dissolved'.[58]

Contrary to some interpretations, Gorz does not glorify domestic labour. His abhorrence of servility, expressed in his critique of commodified personal services, still holds in the case of the unpaid servant – the family member who feels duty-bound and obliged to serve others in relations of domination and subordination which are disguised for what they are in the name of love. Gorz is fully aware of the oppression here – all the more so in the case of women whose activities are restricted to domestic labour in patriarchal households. This is one of the reasons why Gorz believes that work for economic ends in the public sphere is potentially liberating even if it involves the same kinds of tasks carried out in domestic labour. Quite simply, work in the public sphere is legally regulated and frees the worker from personal ties with, and obligations to, an employer. Furthermore,

> The existence of a public contract for the sale of my labour ... designates it as being *labour in general* which is incorporated and incorporates me – into the system of economic and social exchange. It designates me as being a *generally* social, generally useful individual, as capable as anyone else and entitled to the same rights as they are. In other words, it designates me a *citizen*. Paid work in the public sphere therefore constitutes a factor of social insertion.[59]

As an important factor establishing citizenship, work in the economic sense, Gorz emphasises, should not be denied to anyone. However, work in this sense, that is commodity exchange with a recognised social value, 'intended for others as *social*, not private individuals',[60] and performed in the public sphere, is in short supply. As we know, this results in the dualisation of society. The unemployed, temporarily and part-time employed now constitute up to half of the working population in advanced capitalist societies. In other words, up to one half of the working population is denied full citizenship rights. This makes no social sense. Instead we could develop a society in which everyone benefited from the productivity of socialised production, a society in which the whole working population participated in economic activity, and because it (work in an economic sense) is in short supply, everyone could have far more time for work-for-oneself and autonomous activities. It is thus very much an analysis that is continuous with his earlier considerations.

Needs and consumerism

Gorz's analysis of work enables him, by considering the inherent rationalities of different types of human activities, not only to indicate the irrationality of job-creation schemes, thereby debunking the ideology of 'work for work's sake', but also to indicate the irrationality of many existing forms of paid work. The irrationality of the latest forms of job creation, and of some established jobs, which are often based on attempts to commodify the non-commodifiable, derives in part from the inappropriate extension of economic rationality into all spheres of life. It is this, Gorz argues, which is integral to the development of capitalism, and thus to the changing relationship between work, needs and what we consume.[61] Gorz's analysis of work, needs, and consumerism inter-relations is a thoroughly historical one, and one guided by his concern for autonomy – its unnecessary 'repression' and the need for its expansion. The thrust of Gorz's analysis can be grasped by considering:

First, how the capitalist system distances people from their experienced needs, offering 'compensations' for this 'loss' in the form of consumer goods and services. Second, how capitalism's need for consumers translates into socialisation for consumerism, and third, how effective socialisation for consumerism leads to a dependency on commercial products and services, which by their very nature do not match experienced need.

Compensatory consumption In the early days of industrial capitalism profit was to be had in producing for need-based demand. Since then, with the development of capitalism, production has become increasingly distanced from need.

> As productivity and real wages rose during a period of growth, an increasing proportion of the population would have chosen to work less. But workers were never allowed to adjust the hours they put in to the amount of money they felt would take care of their needs. Economic rationality has no room for authentically free time which neither produces nor consumes commercial wealth.[62]

Instead of gaining time for living, time to satisfy the need for autonomy, workers were required to sell more of their labour time than that required to purchase the basic necessities. At the same time, with the realisation that profit from the production for needs is limited, the machinery of socialised production was to be developed in the direction of producing the unnecessary. As Gorz points out, there are limits to the satisfaction of needs, but no such limits exist in the case of desire. Advertisers know this well. But Gorz, like Marcuse,[63] is reluctant to attribute to advertising alone the power to manipulate unnecessary consumption. The consumer, Gorz tells us,

> is not created by capitalism altogether by means of advertising, fashion, and 'human relations', as is often asserted; on the contrary, capitalism *already* creates him within the relationships of production and the work situation by cutting off the producer from his product.[64]

In other words, consumerism has its source in the alienation of labour.

While the socialised production of necessities requires far less labour time than would be the case were we to produce the necessary goods for ourselves, savings in labour time through increasingly efficient production have not been reflected in an equivalent reduction in the working week for full-time employees. A shortened working week would have enabled workers to devote more time to doing things for themselves (work-for-oneself) and to the development of autonomous activities. Loss of time for themselves was compensated by earnings enabling the purchase of superfluous goods. Or, to put it another way, rather than address their own needs for autonomy, workers were compelled to satisfy the capitalists' need for profit.

Gorz notes that trade unions colluded with employers in maintaining an inflated working week.

> To admit that people might actually prefer to work less, although this might mean earning less, and that ultimately everyone might choose their own level of consumption and duration of work, was to admit that wages for full-time work exceeded the level of felt needs for at least part of the working population. Wage claims would thus have lost their legitimacy and, worse, employers might well have wanted to reduce wages if a growing proportion of workers was happy with earning less than what they would be paid for working full-time.[65]

When Gorz refers to workers 'wanting or preferring to work less', he is not distorting history for the sake of his argument. There is a wealth of evidence in support of his claim.[66]

As capitalism has developed, especially since the 1950s, the worker has lost more time to the capitalist system, not by an increase in labour time, but as a consequence of the reshaping of the urban environment to fit the changing requirements of capitalism. Thus, for example, distances between home and work have stretched, and this in a context of declining public transport provision. As early as 1973 Gorz observed: 'The enormous spread of fast cars has effectively increased distances even more rapidly than the speed of the vehicles, and has obliged everyone to devote more time and money, space and energy to travelling.'[67] This example illustrates the fact that capitalism 'creates needs by modifying the conditions under which labour power is reproduced'.[68] The expansion of industrialism, for example, has produced pollution which culminates in individuals being saddled with new health needs. We shall consider this from another angle in due course.

Socialisation for consumerism Capitalism needs consumers. We have already seen how inflated working hours, in reducing the time available in which workers can do more for themselves, steers people towards the consumption of commercially produced goods to satisfy their needs. This is the social reality into which children are born and socialised. The message is clear: 'You work to earn money in order to buy the things you need and want.' This is more likely to be the experience of children than one in which they are surrounded by adults *doing* things for themselves and each other. Advertising, which bombards children via the television screen, merely reinforces the essential message. Children also learn that the achievement of social status, what marks one out from the crowd, is not so much based on what the individual does, but more often than not on what the individual consumes. And, this necessarily means that socialisation for consumerism involves an inculcation of the desire for the superfluous. For it is only in the superfluous that we can differentiate ourselves from others by becoming distinctive consumers.

Distinctive consumption refers 'to the consumption of goods and services of doubtful use value but which, because of their limited availability or high price, confer status or prestige upon those who have access to them'.[69] In many respects producing for distinctive consumption is a major factor fuelling economic growth, *and* a major mechanism in what Illich has termed 'the modernisation of poverty'. Thus Gorz observes that

> once a product enters into common usage, it is time to launch a new product. The product, which is initially scarce and expensive because of its very novelty, enables the rich – independently of all superiority of the new product over the old one – to distinguish themselves *as* rich and to reestablish the poverty of the poor.[70]

By definition, distinctive consumption is irrelevant to the satisfaction of needs, and the orientation of distinctive consumption is matched by the wasteful production of luxury goods, by the wasteful production of the superfluous. Further, since socialisation for consumption is guided by distinctive consumption, there is a sense in which it can be said that socialisation for consumption is a socialisation for distinctive consumption.

Since distinctive consumption is the means through which we are supposed to assert our individuality, it is not surprising that it is part and parcel of capitalism's ideology of individualism. As Gorz notes, 'Advanced capitalism's own model of development … derives from the principle that all problems and needs – even collective ones must be answered by *individual* consumption of marketable goods and services.'[71]

Capitalism not only needs consumers in order to realise profits through the sale of goods and services, but it also needs consumers to carry the burden for its own diseconomies, for example, waste, destruction of the environment, ill-health, and so on. Socialisation for consumerism thus involves the promotion of anti-collectivism by holding the *individual* responsible for the solution of socially caused problems. Yet 'individual solutions are more expensive than a collective response and moreover are increasingly ineffective'.[72]

Gorz has little difficulty in demonstrating this to be the case with evidence pertaining to housing, transport and health. But then, there is more profit to be gained in individual solutions in the form of individual consumption.

Socialisation for consumerism cannot be left to the process of children and young people learning from the example of a consumerist adult world. After all, that example is not a particularly joyous or happy one. If left to their own devices the young might reject following in the footsteps of 'successful' adults – many reject this model anyway. No, matters cannot be left to chance. Somehow individuals have to be made dependent on commercially produced goods and services.

Dependence on consumerism The surest way in which the capitalist system produces consumers is by ensuring that individuals have no time for themselves such that they have no alternative but to buy what they need.[73] The capitalist system not only claims the individual's time through employment and through creating expansionary needs, for example, health, transport, which the individual must address, but also by generating recuperative needs, for example, rest, relaxation, amusement. These needs have become more prominent with the development of dematerialised, mind-numbing, de-skilled work. By administering to these needs, the culture and leisure industries complete the work of the capitalist system in exercising a 'radical monopoly' over people's lives.[74]

As part of their socialisation as consumers, children learn that the passive consumption of entertainment is an established 'reward' for effort. In their own experience it becomes established as a reward for the impositions of 'school work' and its intrusion into free time in the form of homework or studying for exams.

Consumerism feeds off the destruction of our autonomous capacities. The more effective this destruction, the stronger the guarantee that future generations will be so incapable of doing anything for themselves that they will become dependent on marketable goods and services. The destruction of autonomous capacities is, as we saw earlier, a major purpose of normal socialisation. As Gorz says, 'School is the essential machinery for reproducing the social order.' He asks: 'Isn't its function to break spontaneous reactions?'[75] In order to get people to become dependent on consumerism, he argues, they 'have to be kept from satisfying their needs in a spontaneous and independent way'.[76]

Gorz considers a number of consequences of dependency on consumerism. Obviously to satisfy our dependency we need money, which translates into needing paid work. As Gorz puts it: 'The satisfaction afforded by earning money is more important than the loss of freedom entailed by accepting functional work.'[77] This money enables us to meet our basic needs and desires. But does it? Socially produced goods and services are produced for profit, and this necessarily means that they take a standardised form based on prior calculation of profitability. Part of the standardisation process not only involves incorporating superfluousness into the product, but also its planned obsolescence – a major source of future profits. Any satisfaction of needs from purchases is 'by the way' and temporary.

> The citizen no longer consumes those goods and services which correspond to the autonomous needs which he or she feels, but those which correspond to the heteronomous needs attributed to him or her by the professional experts of specialised institutions.[78]

Standardised products are produced with the consumer in mind, not this or that particular person, but a stereotype, that is, as someone belonging to a group attributed with certain standard characteristics. Standardised products are produced for heteronomously defined standard consumers. Up to a half of the populations of Western societies are defined by television controllers, for example, to be of low intelligence, fickle and a little crude. They are thus served up mindless entertainment. Complete dehumanisation awaits totally dependent consumers should they define their own needs, and themselves, in terms of the standardised products available.

Standardised products then, can only match the individual's autonomously defined needs by chance. When we want a car, for example, we do not get an engineer to produce one for our own specifications. We select one from a range of standard models. The individual seeking a gadget-free, easily repairable car, will search in vain. But what of more important needs? Let us consider the effects of standardised medical treatment – standardised as a consequence of the inappropriate application of economic rationality to activities which cannot be measured and monetised. 'If the treatments doctors provide are to be made quantifiable', Gorz argues, 'they must be made to correspond to a standard definition.' Now, this standard, 'a priori definition'

> pre-supposes a standard definition of needs and, therefore, the standardisation of patients. Patients have to correspond to predictable 'cases' that slot readily into a classification table. The GP's first task will thus be to classify the patient: individual consultations and examinations are abandoned in favour of radiography and laboratory tests, advice and explanations are replaced by prescriptions ... The doctor–patient relationship gives way to a purely technical relationship. The *consumption* of

medical services and pharmaceutical products *increases and so does the patients' frustration.*[79]

In this example, which is applicable to attempts to commodify all caring activities, Gorz shows how a caring relationship is transformed into a non-caring one, thereby making it irrelevant to the needs of the patient. Instead of being the recipient of care directed at needs the patient is transformed into being a consumer of products and services reflecting non-caring. To add insult to injury, governments are forever 'assuring' the public that extra expenditure on health services demonstrates their continuing commitment to the provision of 'health care'.

Unfortunately most people in the advanced capitalist societies are totally dependent on a monetised health service. Dependency on consumerism in general, however, is far from total for an increasing proportion of the population. The neat interconnections between work, manipulated needs (substitute needs for the efficient satisfaction of fundamental needs and the substantial satisfactions that ensue from autonomous activities) and consumerism, depicted above, have been broken. Capitalism no longer needs everyone's labour. Experience of intermittent work has forced people, for lack of money, to do more for themselves and to spend time doing things that do not cost money. As a consequence a growing number of individuals have developed a 'critical distancing' from work. This means that these individuals, both the intermittently employed and many full-time workers, no longer identify with their work. This, according to Gorz, signals a cultural change, which prompted him to refer to the emergence of a 'non-class of non-workers' in *Farewell to the Working Class*. This non-class of non-workers constitutes the 'neo-proletariat'.[80]

It is not important what we call people who no longer identify with work. What is more important is that this cultural change is spreading, and that 'the norm to which everyone now refers in his or her actions is no longer the idea of "work", but that of autonomy and self-fulfilment through a freely chosen activity'.[81] If this is true, and we think that it is for a rapidly increasing proportion of the populations of the advanced capitalist societies, then this augurs well for a qualitatively different future in which human activity is based more on the needs of the individual than on the requirements of a system dedicated to profit.

Technology and political ecology

The growing scarcity of full-time employment, which in a sense has 'forced' the intermittently employed to rethink the place of work in their lives, has been caused by capitalism's use of the available technology. Capitalism has always used the technology most likely to deliver the most profit. Until relatively recently the labour made redundant by machinery was re-employed in new areas of socialised industrial production. Until, that is, the invention of the micro-chip in the early 1970s. The use of the micro-chip in industrial production, let alone other kinds of work, has transformed capitalism's labour requirements at a pace that was hitherto inconceivable. Thus Gorz notes that:

> Micro-electronics (of which robots are one applied example) has the previously unheard-of characteristic of making it possible to economise not just on human labour, but on *labour and capital at the same time*. They allow you, if you are an employer, to replace nine-tenths of your workforce with machines – while paying less for these ultra-efficient machines than for the ones you used previously.[82]

Hence investment is reduced, unemployment increases and profits increase. This is what the advanced capitalist societies have been experiencing for the past twenty years. This process cannot go on indefinitely because capitalism might run out of consumers. Hence recent job-creation schemes, for example, in personal services, where workers are paid for useless work in order that they can consume.

Automation not only gets rid of jobs, it also gets rid of skills. 'Automation and computerisation have eliminated most skills and possibilities for initiative and are in the process of replacing what remains of the skilled labour force (whether blue or white collar) by a new type of unskilled worker.'[83] De-skilled work is meaningless work, especially so when the worker is an appendage of some pre-programmed machine. The choice facing intermittent workers today is that between seeking futile work, as a 'new servant' for example,[84] and heteronomous meaningless work, which boils down to the same thing. Thus the 'technologicalisation' of work has contributed massively to the inability of workers to identify with 'their' work.

The central significance of technological developments, under current social arrangements, is that of 'forcing' individuals to seek meaning outside of paid work. This, of course, is the significance of the cultural change which Gorz has been addressing since the publication of *Farewell to the Working Class*. If we are to believe the prevailing sociological orthodoxy, then it would seem that people seek meaning, and can achieve it, through consumerism.[85] Gorz's understanding of consumerism, as we have seen, suggests that the sociological orthodoxy is at best superficial, and at worst wrong. There is no need to repeat his arguments here. We can embellish them by merely asking: if consumerism supplies people with meaning, why is it that in the consumer paradises of the affluent societies millions of people experience crises of meaning?[86] But, even if we concede that some individuals gain some kind of meaning from consumerism, is this available to those without excess money? In other words, is it available to the intermittently employed? It would seem that for the majority of these people consumerism is not the answer to their need for a meaningful life.

Paraphrasing the conclusions of a life satisfaction study, Gorz notes that 'consumption and the money which makes it possible ... only have a tenuous link with the things that make people happy: autonomy, self-esteem, a happy family life, the absence of conflicts in life outside work, friendship'.[87] Gorz goes on to argue that the 'quality of life depends on the intensity of human bonds and cultural exchanges, relations built on friendship, love, brother- and sisterhood and mutual aid, and not on the intensity of commodity relations'.[88]

The significance of these observations resides in the fact that our most meaningful experiences do not require money. They do require time and a supportive culture. While cultural support is underdeveloped, one necessary resource for its development, time, is available for the intermittently employed. The cultural change which has been brought about by capitalism's use of micro-electronic technology has pushed the intermittently employed in a direction compatible with what Gorz terms 'ecological rationalisation'.

> Ecological rationalisation can be summed up in the slogan 'less but better'. Its aim is a society in which we live better while working and consuming less. Ecological modernisation requires that investment no longer serve the growth of the economy but its contraction ... There can be no ecological modernisation without restricting the dynamic of capitalist accumulation and reducing consumption by self-imposed restraint. The exigencies of ecological modernisation coincide with those of a transformed North–South relationship, and with the original aims of socialism.[89]

Even before Gorz wrote the essays that make up *Ecology as Politics* he was highly critical of the environmental destruction produced as a consequence of industrial growth. In *Ecology as Politics* Gorz drew on the kind of thinking reflected in the Club of Rome's depiction of ecological crisis[90] and the more theoretically informed writings of Ivan Illich,[91] to radicalise his critique of capitalism. At one level, the more superficial one, Gorz's writings on ecological crisis can be seen as illustrative of the now familiar analysis of all the ways in which economic growth via industrialism is not sustainable forever. Quite simply, growing industrial production uses up finite resources, depletes vital resources such as soil damaged and lost as a consequence of the methods of agribusiness, and air and water as a consequence of the polluting effects of industrial waste and energy consumption. Also familiar, at least to ecologists, is the argument that economic growth and consumerism are inextricably linked, and therefore halting growth in order to preserve the planet for supporting life will involve a radical change in the consumerist lifestyles of the affluent.

At another level, the deeper one, Gorz's focus on the effects of ecological crisis can be seen as a form of empirical evidence illustrating his comprehensive critique of capitalism. His analysis of the manipulation of consumer needs goes further than anything available in the ecological literature. The same can be said for his analysis of the way in which industrial capitalism, in order to reproduce itself, 'costs more than it yields. In other words, *industry consumes more for its own needs:* it delivers fewer products to the final consumer than it used to. Its efficiency has diminished; its physical costs have increased.'[92]

In saying this we are claiming that Gorz's ecological writings are not solely represented in *Ecology as Politics*, and in *Capitalism, Socialism, Ecology. All* of his writings since *Ecology as Politics* are ecological. This is not to say that they are not socialist – they most certainly are. But it is to say that they are ecological by virtue of the fact that they constitute the most comprehensively radical critique of economic rationality around, not to save capitalism from itself, but to point us beyond capitalism to a future in which we can live more harmoniously with nature and with our 'bodily' autonomous selves. *Critique of Economic Reason* is thus, in our view, Gorz's major contribution to the ecology movement.

It is since *Ecology as Politics* that Gorz has clearly made the distinction between his own approach (what he refers to as 'political ecology') and environmentalism or what he sometimes refers to as 'scientific ecology'. Essentially the latter fails to challenge economic rationality centred on the aim of continuous economic growth. As such, revelations of environmental damage can be readily used by the capitalist system. This system is already adept at transforming diseconomies into calculations of economic growth without raising productivity – as in the case of environmentally caused illnesses being a source of profit for drug companies. Gorz elaborates:

> Destruction officially appears as a source of wealth since the replacement of everything broken, thrown out or lost gives rise to new production, sales, monetary flows and profits. The more quickly things are broken, worn out, made obsolete or thrown away, the larger the GNP will be and the wealthier the national statistics will say we are. Even illness and physical injury are

presented as sources of wealth, for they swell the consumption of drugs and health-care facilities.[93]

Forms of environmental cleansing, such as the recycling industry and the production of environmentally friendly goods, merely extend the very system which has created the need for them.

By contrast, Gorz's political ecology 'challenges the reasons behind the development of a certain number of technologies, products, and forms of consumption in the first place. These reasons are contained in the logic of capitalist accumulation.'[94] The aims of political ecology are 'to reduce the sphere in which economic rationality and commodity exchanges apply, and to subordinate it to non-quantifiable societal and cultural ends and to the free development of individuals'.[95]

Capitalism/socialism

For Gorz, political ecology and socialism are part and parcel of each other. Both are in conflict with capitalism. Thus he argues that: 'What is at stake in the conflict between capitalism and socialism is not economic rationality as such, but the extent of the sphere in which economic rationality may exert its effects.'[96] Now, as we have seen earlier, particularly in Gorz's analysis of work and consumption, *'Capitalism has been the expression of economic rationality finally set free of all restraint.'*[97] In recent times the pursuit of profit has extended economic rationality into inappropriate spheres, rendering it irrational. 'Whole areas of economic life now have the sole function of "providing work", or of producing for the sake of keeping people working.' Society's 'chief objective' under these circumstances, is 'simply "to keep people occupied", and thereby to preserve the relations of subordination'.[98] As the irrational extension of economic rationality continues, as when 'consumers are paid to consume and producers are a minority', it becomes increasingly evident that contemporary capitalism is not solely concerned with production for profit, but equally with control and domination. 'Production system and control system become one and the same.'[99] Gorz had already established this in his analysis of the division of labour.

> It is this *domination* by economic rationality, embodied in capital and its techno-bureaucratic apparatuses, which defines capitalism, not the existence of an economic sphere governed by the logic of profitability and competition. It is the abolition of that domination, not the abolition of capital and the market, which will mark our passing beyond capitalism.[100]

It is this domination, what Habermas refers to as 'the colonisation of the lifeworld',[101] which has proven to be a socially disintegrating force, rendering traditional norms and values irrelevant and has created an asocial society devoid of communality. It is this domination which has severely restricted the expression of autonomy and the achievement of a meaningful and satisfying life. So, if we are to move beyond capitalism towards a society which removes this domination it will be necessary not only to restrict the sphere of economic rationality, but also to reclaim the lifeworld, to create the social and cultural conditions supportive of autonomy and fulfilment. 'Socialism,' Gorz writes, 'may, therefore, be understood as the positive response to the disintegration of social bonds ensuing from the commodity and competitive relations characteristic of capitalism.'[102]

> A society becomes socialist when the social relations shaped by the economic rationality of capital come to occupy only a subordinate place in relation to non-quantifiable values and goals, and in consequence, in the life of society and in each person's life, economically rational work is merely one activity among others of equal importance.[103]

The *distinctiveness* of Gorz's socialism can be highlighted by briefly indicating its difference from the Soviet model on the one hand, and the social-democratic welfarist model on the other. In the former model the worker was to achieve self-realisation through work contributing to the 'common good'. The collective ownership and control of the means of production would enable this to happen. Self-interest and collective interest were to become one and the same thing, and would be embodied within The Plan. The whole society would benefit equally from the distribution of the fruits of everyone's labour. Gorz provides a number of reasons why this model, in practice, has failed to realise its intent. More importantly, however, 'the underlying reason for its failure is ontological: the Marxian utopia by which functional work and personal activity could be made to coincide is ontologically unrealizable *on the scale of large systems*'.[104] In elaborating on this Gorz refers us to his analysis of heteronomy.

> In order to function, the industrial-bureaucratic megamachine requires a subdivision of tasks which, once put into effect, is self-perpetuating and *has to be* self-perpetuating by inertia, if the functional capacity of each of its human cogs is to be made reliable and calculable. The definition and distribution of these partial tasks are thus determined by the material matrix ... of the megamachine whose functioning they are to ensure. It is strictly impossible subsequently to reinterpret this functionalisation of

hetero-determined activities in terms of voluntary social collaboration.[105]

Workers' experience of functional work provides insufficient knowledge of the workings of the total system of production. How can they possibly engage in any planning of socialised production? In practice, those with the necessary knowledge will be those distanced from the specific 'hands-on' experience of the worker. Whether it be party or state or some other body, The Plan will necessarily be conceived at least at one remove from the worker. Instead of workers' control, we have workers' subordination to an imposed plan – imposed by those by virtue of their function in the collective order.

> Because it was divorced from the intuitive understanding of their surroundings and relations with one another of which individuals were capable, this methodically programmed rationalisation established Reason as a separate power exercised *over* them and not *by* them and established the realm of Reason as the dictatorial rule of those who, as a result of their functions, were its custodians.[106]

The rest is history.

Gorz's socialism retains the laudable aims of this Marxist model. He is intent on subordinating the economy to political control, to place it in the service of society. But the control of the economy is to be focused on delimiting the sphere of economic rationality rather than workers controlling production by exercising control at the sites of production – even if it was possible, which it is not. Besides, the idea of attempting to control the sites of production is meaningless given the hetero-determined nature of functional work in vast, complex systems of production. With this being the case, what kind of freedom would it be? Liberation in the form of freedom to determine functional, meaningless work, is a nonsense. Surely liberation is better served by freeing oneself from functional work. This, for Gorz, is the main purpose of limiting the economic sphere. In other words, liberation is to be found in an expanded sphere of autonomy outside of work.

In rejecting Soviet-style socialism, Gorz does not opt for the social-democratic alternative centred on the redistribution of wealth in the form of state provision of welfare and public services. The welfarist model of socialism, argues Gorz, is no socialism at all. At best it is a 'humanised capitalism',[107] '*a substitute for society*'.[108] Gorz appreciates that the role of the state in capitalist societies is a complex one. It intervenes in the economy through regulation, taxes, subsidies, and so on, for 'left to itself, the market economy always evolves inexorably towards collapse'.[109] It responds to collective needs which tend to be ignored by the market through the provision of public and welfare services. And it responds to individual needs for security in a system that continuously generates this need. Yet within capitalism these functions, however useful they might be to the stability of the capitalist system as a whole, are in conflict with individual enterprises each attempting to gain advantage against each other. Furthermore the provision of public and welfare services by the state is dependent on the taxation of profits.

The very need for the provision of public and welfare services has arisen as a consequence of the development of capitalism, particularly the disintegration of civil society. It is thus somewhat perverse to identify socialism with the expansion of these services. This has been and still is the aim of many self-proclaimed socialists working within social-democratic political parties. In other words the expansion of public and welfare services is intended to create socialist 'enclaves in the heart of economic rationality', but importantly, 'without in any way limiting its domination over society. These enclaves, on the contrary', are 'dependent on the good working of capitalism and intended to promote it'.[110]

Not only is the welfarist route to socialism a non-starter in the basic sense that it does not go beyond capitalism, but administered services, no matter how extensive, do not promote lived forms of sociability and solidarity. In other words, administered services fall a long way short of the socialist ideal of collective self-determination.

> They merely compensate for the decay, brought about by market and commodity relations, of grass-roots communities and of social cohesion anchored in the lifeworld, and thereby accelerate both that decay and an ever greater spread of commodity and cash relationships. The welfare state becomes the guardian of the general interest against the 'every man for himself' of market society, and also promotes the latter, in that it takes over and administers the general interest as an instance separated from civil society.[111]

It needs to be made clear at this point that Gorz is not advocating the abolition of the welfare state. He is simply arguing that socialism cannot be achieved as a consequence of the development of the welfare state. In 'redefining socialism' Gorz is adamant that it

> must not be conceived of as a different economic and social *system*. Quite the contrary: it is the conscious practical project of abolishing everything that makes society a system, a megamachine, together with the simultaneous expansion of autonomous self-regulated forms of sociability, which make possible 'the free development of individuality'.[112]

But this does not mean abolishing planning. Gorz is fully aware that the regulatory powers of nation-states have become more difficult to exercise with the growing internationalisation of capital.[113] Clearly, international regulation is required – but not in the form typically adopted by the nation-state. If economic rationality is to be confined to its appropriate sphere, if it is to serve society, then society itself must do the required planning.

> The point is to subject economic and technical development to a pattern and orientations which have been thought through and democratically debated; to tie in the goals of the economy with the free public expression of felt needs, instead of creating needs for the sole purpose of enabling capital to expand and commerce to develop.[114]

In short, planning should be a thoroughly democratic process, and, for us in Europe, it should forge policies on a European scale.

So, for Gorz socialist politics 'cannot be content merely to correct and regulate the operation of the market ... It must promote *the social control of markets by citizens working together, and not merely by the public authorities*.'[115]

> The question of what must be produced and how, the question of social priorities, of models of consumption, of styles of life – all this is currently decided by technocrats, businessmen and bankers. Socialism would have to mean the democratisation of these decisions, their public discussion at the level of associations, trade unions, movements, public hearings, and elected assemblies; and it would also have to mean taking into account criteria with which technocrats and company directors do not normally concern themselves.[116]

The big question is how can such a socialist politics materialise? Gorz's answer to this question is to be found in his politics of time.

The politics of time

From *Farewell to the Working Class* onwards, Gorz's books have promoted a *practical* politics based on the emancipatory potential of reduced working hours. As he says,

> In the future, the Left will mainly be distinguished from the Right by the emancipatory goals towards which it seeks to guide technical change ... It will be distinguished from the Right by its will to use savings in time for societal and cultural ends, which will regulate economic objectives to the second rank.[117]

Gorz is in the habit of reminding us that in the advanced capitalist societies we are increasingly producing more and more with decreasing amounts of labour time. And he is forever supporting this fact with the latest statistics. Thus in *Farewell to the Working Class* Gorz informs us that throughout this century 'productivity (i.e. output per hour of work) has risen twelvefold. Since 1936 and the law establishing a 40-hour week in France it has almost quadrupled. But the number of working hours has not fallen noticeably.'[118] Just over ten years later Gorz presents us with the fact that:

> In the capitalist countries of Europe, taken as a whole, three to four times more wealth is produced today than thirty-five years ago. But it does not take three times more hours of work to achieve this more than tripled level of production. It requires a much lower quantity.[119]

We have already seen how Gorz uses such statistics to support his analysis and critique of economic rationality. But what is essential in understanding his advocacy of an emancipatory politics of time is the particular use of these statistics in this regard. Gorz argues that these statistics reflect a trend (or, more substantially, a direction) that is likely to continue for the foreseeable future. In other words we now know that the productivity of each unit of labour will continue to increase, that is, less labour time will be required to produce the same volume of goods next year compared to this year. Given that micro-electronic technology has yet to invade all areas of productive activity, Gorz is surely correct in his assumption. Because we know now that productivity will increase we do, in theory, have the choice of deciding what to do with the saved labour time. But in order to materialise this theoretical choice, we need an effective politics of time.

It is a relatively easy matter to advocate this or that kind of politics. There is no shortage of ideas about what needs to be done. It is however quite another matter to transform these ideas into policies that are *practically* feasible. If we are sympathetic to Gorz's social critique we will be convinced of the desirability of an expanded sphere of autonomy. But Gorz does not let things rest there. He offers us a practical way forward. Herein resides the ingenuity of the manner of his reasoning with respect to future savings in labour time. His reasoning is a radical departure from reasoning 'ex post, ... that is, starting out from a situation which is the final outcome of a *past* development'. Gorz continues:

> From this point of view, the die is already cast: the fruits of economic growth and productivity gains have always *already been shared out*. They cannot be distributed a second time, between a greater number of people, without reducing the share each person receives.

But what seems impossible retrospectively becomes possible if we reason *ex ante* on the best way to allocate the fruits of a development that is *yet to come*. The division of the spoils then becomes a matter of political decision as to how the future is to be shaped.[120]

In other words 'reduction of work time ... should not be the result of productivity increases, but their goal and driving force'.[121]

All of this implies the democratisation of economic decision-making, and especially a pro-active role for trade unions, not only at the level of each enterprise, but also in the determination of a society-wide (European) policy. Gorz does address his proposals to trade unionists.[122] He urges them to look beyond the protection of the particular interests of their own unions, and to take up a politics of time. This is not to say that a successful politics of time will endanger the trade unions. Gorz makes it quite clear that all will benefit. Failure to develop a politics of time will mean that the capitalist system will continue to reproduce the dual society, will continue to use high levels of unemployment to impose discipline in the workplace and to depress wages, and will continue to generate useless, low-paid jobs. The very existence of the dual society,which characterises the advanced capitalist societies today, is reason enough to develop a politics of time. But Gorz does not rest his case here. The case for a politics of time is strengthened by his discussion of the main issues to be addressed in formulating a policy of reduced working hours. Such a policy implies 'basic choices about what kind of society we are going to live in'.[123]

In discussing these choices Gorz presents the preferences of those on the right among others, demonstrating both their ideological, sectional nature, and their disregard for society as a whole. He thus notes that 'until now, the length of working time has been reduced in an extremely differentiated manner; for some workers it has fallen to zero; for others, it has not changed'. This is unsatisfactory, as too are proposals for 'less extreme forms of differentiation'. Gorz's objections are based on his commitment to equality and justice. In presenting a possible emancipatory alternative, Gorz does not engage in a heavy bout of philosophical argument – he merely appeals to our sense of justice.

One of the functions of a politics of time is precisely to share out savings in working time following principles not of economic rationality but of justice. These savings are the work of society as a whole. The political task is to redistribute them on the scale of society as a whole so that each man and woman can benefit from them.[124]

Consistent with this principle, Gorz states that the 'two inseparable objectives' of an emancipatory politics of time are:

> (a) that everyone should work less, so that everyone may work and may also develop outside their working lives the personal potential which cannot find expression in their work; (b) that a much greater proportion of the population should be able to have access to skilled, complex, creative and responsible occupational activities which allow them continually to develop and grow.[125]

With respect to this second objective, Gorz notes that it is in the more skilled professions that gains in productivity have been smaller and slower, and thus a society-wide reduction in working time would allow more people to work in these professions. This would enable 'areas of competence monopolised by elitist bodies to be democratised'.[126] Gorz recognises that objections to this are likely to come from the professions most intent on safeguarding their elite status. Professionals and occupational elites tend to argue that the nature of their work is such, that to be successful long working hours are necessary. Gorz shows this kind of argument to be a bogus one on *practical* grounds.

> It is not true that continuous relentless application to one's work leads to professional success and creativity. The more skilled a type of work, the more time the people who do it need to spend updating their knowledge, trying out new ideas, and allowing themselves to remain open-minded and receptive by diversifying their interests.[127]

Gorz concludes that 'working less (in terms of the number of hours devoted directly to one's occupation) means working better, especially in innovative or continually evolving jobs'.[128]

The greater the democratisation of jobs the greater will be the possibility of 'self-managed' working time, thereby enabling individuals to fit in their periods of work with their own priorities. Gorz's advocacy of self-managed working time is thus consistent with the emancipatory goal of subordinating the sphere of heteronomy to the sphere of autonomy. Additionally, however, it makes *practical* sense.

> If the object is to spread a decreasing volume of work out among an increasing (or even a constant) number of people, it is practically impossible that they should all be present at the place of work on the same days and at the same hours.[129]

Thus far we have seen that Gorz's politics of time trades on the existential appeal of greater autonomy, our sense of justice, and, as we have emphasised, a strong practical sense. 'But,' the sceptic might say, 'Gorz seems to ignore the very likely possibility that those in full-time jobs will not want to work less if it means earning less. This alone indicates that Gorz is thoroughly impractical, and that his politics of time cannot possibly get off the ground.' Such a view can only be advanced by those who have failed to grasp the significance of a *policy* of reduced working hours which is decided *ex-ante* and not *ex-post*. *Ex-ante* planning, Gorz has demonstrated in both *Critique of Economic Reason* and *Capitalism, Socialism, Ecology*, enables (if we want it) the reduction of working hours and an increase in earnings and an increase in employment.[130]

How does Gorz demonstrate this possibility? Slightly underestimating recent rates of economic growth and productivity gains, Gorz projects them four years ahead. The exact figures are of little consequence to Gorz's demonstration, but to use his example, he has projected that 'in four years, production will have increased by 8 per cent and productivity by 12 per cent'. This means that in order 'to produce 108 per cent of the current volume of disposable wealth, a quantity of labour of just 96 per cent will be needed (100+8–12)'. Four options are available:

1. We can *maintain current working hours* which has the effect of more unemployment (4 per cent of the workforce) and earnings can increase by 12 per cent. As Gorz says, 'This is roughly what has happened in industry during the recent period.'
2. We can *maintain employment at current levels*, which, because 'they produce 8 per cent more in 4 per cent fewer hours, enables wages to go up by 8 per cent and working hours to go down by 4 per cent'.
3. We can *maintain wages at current levels*, which would allow us to employ 8 per cent more while reducing working hours by 12 per cent.
4. We can *reduce working hours while increasing wages and the workforce*. Given the calculations within each of the first three options, it is clear that (theoretically) we do have the choice of mixing up the variables (working hours, wages and workforce) in a variety of ways. Thus,

   We could, for example, employ 5 per cent more workers, increase wages on average by 3 per cent and reduce working hours by 9 per cent ... If we employ 6 per cent more people, working hours can be reduced by 10 per cent and wages increased by 2 per cent.[131]

So, it is possible to reduce working hours while increasing wages and the workforce. But is it desirable? Gorz's preference is that we work toward zero economic growth (for obvious ecological reasons). He calculates a number of alternative scenarios given no more than a 9 per cent rise in productivity over four years.[132] But realistically, Gorz believes that his politics of time has a better chance of succeeding if a little growth is planned. He explains:

> Choosing zero growth means, in fact, that a third of all job-holders – those at the top of the scale – who are also the most influential politically and culturally will have to accept reductions in their purchasing power. These reductions will not easily be accepted, since it will be necessary not only to maintain or even improve the real incomes of the workers at the bottom of the scale but also to raise the general level of skills and qualifications, and increase the proportion of highly skilled jobs.[133]

While Gorz has his own theoretically embedded preferences, he is not naive enough to suppose that they can find clear practical application in a reality which does not altogether conform to his own thinking. He thus asks: 'Can we expect the most skilled workers alone to suffer the drawbacks of a policy of RWH (reduced working hours) *before they have even been able to discover its advantages*?' His answer is, 'I do not believe so.'[134] Hence the planning of a little growth initially.

Before looking at the major benefits of reduced working hours, it is necessary to note that a planned, staged reduction of working hours, while increasing the workforce without loss of income, will require financing. One cannot expect efficient enterprises to compensate their workers for the hours they no longer work – this would defeat the purpose of efficiency. Neither can one expect the compensation to be funded by taxing individual incomes. What Gorz does propose is compensation in the form of an indirect income paid out of a separate public fund, which is formed by a tax on consumption.[135] The tax could be imposed at a variable rate to reflect the use-value of different goods. Luxury items, for example, would attract a higher rate of tax.

The indirect income, or 'second cheque', is not to be confused with the variety of proposals known as guaranteed minimum income (GMI) schemes. Many of these schemes have been advocated by the right as an alternative to current welfare arrangements. Gorz is highly critical of such schemes.

> The guarantee of an income independent of a job will be emancipatory or repressive ... according to whether it opens up new spaces for individual and *social activity* or whether, on the contrary, it is only the social wage for compulsory passivity.

Gorz stresses the point that 'the guarantee of an income independent of a job will only bring freedom if it is accompanied by the *right to work for everyone*'.[136] This is particularly important. This is why the reduction of working hours is so crucial. A state-provided grant (guaranteed income) for the unemployed implies the continuing reinforcement of the existence of individuals who are superfluous to society, whereas the reduction of working hours can lead to a situation in which all can perform socially useful work. And, Gorz argues, the 'indissoluble unity of the right to an income and the right to work is the basis of citizenship for every man and woman'.[137] As a citizen, the individual is 'of society', belongs to society, and is thus obliged to do what is socially necessary. 'There can be no rights without corresponding obligations.'[138] Obligations and rights form a dialectical unity. Thus the right to work, and to an income for socially recognised work are underpinned by our obligation to society.

> The essential aspect of an obligation to work in exchange for a guaranteed full income is that this obligation provides the basis for a corresponding right: by obliging individuals to produce by working the income which is guaranteed to them, society obliges itself to guarantee them the opportunity to work and gives them the right to demand this. The obligation it imposes on them is the basis for the right they have over it, the right to be full citizens.[139]

Gorz's politics of time is the practical culmination of his thinking. It is, however, an open-ended culmination in so far as his proposals indicate crucial areas of decision-making, and are a stimulus for democratic involvement. With respect to the redistribution of jobs which a politics of time entails, Gorz argues that 'it is one of the specific aims of an RWH policy to render ... collective bargaining necessary'.

> Announcing several years in advance that working hours will be substantially reduced at a set date is an extraordinarily effective lever for mobilizing society for what is simultaneously a challenge, an opportunity, a goal and a springboard towards new changes. The stakes for the workers and the interest they can take in this are far more stimulating than anything quality circles have to offer. All the aspects of working conditions are now up for grabs.[140]

Gorz's proposals must not be seen as a blueprint. Indeed, they cannot be a blueprint for the simple reason that once people have experienced the benefits of reduced working hours it is most likely that the nature and intensity of their demands and expectations will change. What are these benefits? Those who are intermittently employed or more or less permanently unemployed will gain the security which current arrangements undermine. Those in full-time employment will gain time. Time is not only essential for autonomous activities, but the lack of it is the major cause of 'the exploding demand for institutionalised services'.

> Parents no longer have enough time for their children, nor the young for the old, the healthy for the sick or the able-bodied for the handicapped. As a result, babies are sent to day-care centres, the old to old-people's homes, the handicapped to special centres, 'maladjusted' pupils to special classes where they stagnate for ever, and so on.[141]

More time would clearly reduce the demand for institutionalised services, since the work could be done by people for themselves, and this in turn would demand less expenditure from individual incomes, which in turn, could form the basis for planning zero growth with more radical reductions in working hours. This is just one example of the dynamic nature of a policy of reduced working hours.

However, Gorz does warn us that these benefits are far more likely if the self-management of work time is handled in a way which allows individuals vast tracts of continuous free time. Working one hour a day less, for example, perpetuates the fragmentation of time and is thus likely to maintain patterns of time-use. Fragmented time is, of course, the target of the leisure and entertainment industries. The latter especially promotes our passivity rather than the development of our autonomous capacities.

How we manage our work time will determine the usefulness, and thus the benefits of increased free time. At least equally important though (and this is an essential part of Gorz' politics of time) an RWH policy must be accompanied by:

1. A politics of collective facilities, which can provide cities, towns and even apartment blocks with places for communication, interchange and autonomous activity ... [and]
2. A politics of voluntary co-operation and association allowing the development of all kinds of local, non-market, collective services, which are more effective, more appropriate and more adaptable, as well as being less expensive, when they are not state-run institutions: child-care co-ops, shared transport, help for the elderly. At least part of the money thus saved by the state would be given to these informal co-ops.[142]

It is just these politics that are supportive of the development of sociality, mutuality and solidarity that are, along with more autonomy, essential ingredients of a quality of life that is all but denied in a society dominated by commodity relations. Experiencing the substantial satisfactions that derive from such a quality of life contributes to the dynamic processes unleashed by a politics of time. 'The more people are capable of practical and affective autonomy, the less they are willing to accept hierarchical discipline and the more demanding they become as regards both the quality and the content of the work required of them.'[143]

Finally it can be noted that the manner in which Gorz proposes that the sphere of heteronomy is to be subordinated to the sphere of autonomy, the realm of economic rationality to political decisions reflecting needs, does reduce the demand for the consumption of goods and services. The self-limitation of needs in his scheme of things is a limitation *without* experienced deprivation. And, it is a limitation that not only satisfies the requirements of political ecology, but one that can transform the relations between the affluent world and the Third World.

> The solution to the specific problems of the under-nourished world depends on the industrialised world adopting a model of consumption and production that is less wasteful, less ostentatious, and which generates less dependence, enabling people to be more capable of producing what they consume.[144]

But, if Gorz's future is to be realised one can expect a long, hard struggle against the forces of capital. The latter will resist any attempts to move in the direction proposed by Gorz. Quite simply, reduced demand for profitable goods and services spells disaster for the capitalist system. Additionally, the prospect of populations unleashing and developing their autonomy cannot be tolerated by a system whose very reproduction is based on controlling people. No doubt it is considerations such as these that underpin the view that Gorz's proposals for RWH are unrealistic. Yet these same kinds of views were expressed with respect to similar proposals that have since become established. As Gorz argues:

> The six-day week and the eight-hour day were originally regarded as ruinous demands ... At the beginning of the century, full-time employment meant working more than three thousand hours a year. In 1960, the figure was twenty-one hundred. In 1985, it was sixteen hundred hours.[145]

Of course, it is possible to realise Gorz's proposals. But we will have to fight for them.

4

Gorz and His Critics

Understandably, given the range of themes in Gorz's work, he does get mentioned a lot in academic literature, though the academic world has yet to develop a standard reception of Gorz. He does pose a difficulty for those academics who are in the habit of classifying thought. As we have seen, Gorz's thinking has been developed as a consequence of addressing problems experienced by the mass of people in their everyday lives. He has drawn on existentialism, anarcho-syndicalism, humanistic Marxism, Illich, and his thinking does bear some similarities with the critical theory of Marcuse.[1] Needless to say, Gorz's thinking cannot be reduced to any one tradition. He cannot be pigeonholed. Any attempts to do so are meaningless.[2]

The coverage of Gorz's work in academic texts varies in length, the author's intent, and most importantly in quality. We are in total agreement with Finn Bowring who has demonstrated that 'Gorz is widely misrepresented and significantly misunderstood'.[3] In some cases the reading of Gorz is so slipshod that blatant errors are generated. Of course some errors are of little consequence. Such is the case, for example, with Chris Whitbread's claim that the concept of autonomy/heteronomy is 'absent from his 1980 collection *Ecology as Politics*, it … doesn't come from Illich'.[4] Gorz does use the autonomy/heteronomy distinction in *Ecology as Politics*, and it does come from Illich.[5]

More serious are those errors that appear in textbooks in which the student might expect to find accurate coverage of Gorz's work. In a widely used introductory sociology textbook, for example, we are told that Gorz presents us with a view of leisure in industrial society in which the individual is nothing more than 'a mindless "happy robot" compulsively chasing "false needs"'.[6] Not only is this just plainly wrong, Gorz actually sets out to argue as such. Apparently, according to this textbook writer, Gorz shares this view with Marcuse. In fact, Gorz tells us that this is a point of disagreement between him and Marcuse. Later we are told that Gorz argues that 'the capitalist controlled mass media, with its advertisements that proclaim the virtues of family life and associate the products of industry with those virtues, simply creates "false needs"'.[7] Again, this is wrong.

Similar errors surface in more specialised textbooks, in which the student might expect to find a non-superficial coverage of Gorz. Thus, amid a catalogue of errors, Chris Rojek asserts that one of Gorz's 'most sociologically questionable' assumptions is 'that post-industrial socialism will be run on the lines of the *full collectivization* of the means of production'.[8] Rojek does not seem to have read the second chapter of *Farewell to the Working Class*. It is here that Gorz makes it abundantly clear that his own model of socialism is developed in part via an extensive critique of the idea of 'the *full collectivization* of the means of production'.

It is safe to assume, however, that the serious Gorz scholar is likely to consult 'more advanced' sources which contain critical discussion of Gorz's work. In this event the student needs to be alerted to two standard academic practices, which in conjunction with misrep-resentation, can transform critical discussion into an irrelevance.

The first of these practices involves the articulation of the critic's own position under the guise of criticism of a book or theorist. It is normally the case that the ensuing 'criticism' reveals more about the critic than about the object of criticism. An obvious example is Murray Bookchin's critique of *Ecology as Politics*. Bookchin criticises Gorz for his (Gorz's) failure to adopt his (Bookchin's) distinction between ecology and environmentalism. It is fair to say that Gorz could be a little clearer in his own rendition of 'two kinds of ecology', but it is not valid to criticise him because he is not Bookchin.

Bookchin's 'critique' of Gorz is essentially a vehicle for Bookchin to express his strong distaste of Marxism and socialism, and thus his opposition to any attempt to develop an ecologically sensitive socialism. Bookchin asserts that 'the Marxian corpus lies in an uncovered grave, distended by gases and festering with molds and worms'.[9] Having identified Gorz as a Marxist – an orthodox, if incompetent, one at that – Bookchin finds Gorz an easy target for abuse. He is obviously afraid that *Ecology as Politics*, like all forms of libertarian Marxism, might exert a destructive influence on the libertarianism of the ecology movement. Bookchin accuses both Marcuse and Gorz of 'ideological obscurantism' for 'their repeated attempts to reformulate *both* sides of the issue: the old socialist categories and the new libertarian ones'. Bookchin warns that 'the result that inevitably follows is that the logic of each is warped and its inherent opposition to the other is blurred'.[10] And, this 'result' is what is destructive! Gorz's *Strategy for Labour*, according to Bookchin,

> by miscasting students and intellectuals as a 'new proletariat,' deflected the growing insight of sixties' radicals from *cultural* movements into classical economistic ones, producing massive

confusion in the American student movement of the time. More than any single journalistic work, this book brought Marxism into the Students for a Democratic Society, producing the ideological chaos that eventually destroyed it.[11]

Former members of the Students for a Democratic Society (SDS) would be justified in finding these remarks patronising. Now, what happened to the SDS can, Bookchin fears, happen to the ecology movement if it listens to Gorz.

> His recent *Ecology and Freedom* (retitled *Ecology as Politics*) is essentially the *New Strategy for Labour* writ in ecological verbiage. It perpetuates all the incompatibilities of a mythic 'libertarian socialism' that sprinkles anarchist concepts of decentralized organization with Social Democratic concepts of mass political parties and, more offensively, 'radical ecology' with the opportunistic politics of conventional environmentalism.[12]

In fact, *Ecology as Politics* 'perpetuates a confusion that has already produced an internal crisis in every American and European ecology movement'.[13] This 'crisis', for Bookchin, has been caused by the influence of Marxism. Had Gorz adopted Bookchin's distinction between environmentalism and social ecology, he would have had

> to confront the serious challenges a radical social ecology raises to his *own* mode of thinking – notably, *socialist* 'thinking'. For the real conflict that faces the Left so far as society and the natural world is concerned *is not between a specious form of bourgeois 'ecology' and socialist politics but between a libertarian form of social ecology and an economistic, technologically orientated form of socialism – in short, Marxism.*[14]

Bookchin does seem to have a problem. Enough said.

The second standard academic practice that can generate irrelevant criticism can be referred to as superfluous academic production. Essentially the critic misreads a theorist, for example, and then proceeds to criticise the theorist as if the misreading is in fact a truthful reading. Sean Sayers, for example, tells us that Gorz provides 'no criteria for deciding where – if anywhere, the economic rationalisation of housework is appropriate'.[15] Not only is Sayers wrong since Gorz does provide explicit criteria, but strangely Sayers acknowledges as much in a footnote, but proceeds to criticise Gorz on the basis of his not providing the criteria. As we shall see throughout this chapter, much of what passes as criticism does adopt this practice.

While much criticism of Gorz can be rejected out of hand, there is, nevertheless, value in addressing criticisms that may help to clarify our understanding of Gorz. In the remainder of this chapter we will dwell on the main issues raised by, for the most part, the more informed of Gorz's critics. These issues are: Gorz's (mis)representation of Marx; the concept of the neo-proletariat; the value of Gorz's distinction between the spheres of heteronomy and autonomy in a future socialism; Gorz's alleged sexism; Gorz's alleged ethnocentricism; Gorz's tendency to 'exaggerate' the significance of 'cultural trends' and social changes, and Gorz's (lack of a) political strategy.

Gorz's (mis)representation of Marx

By its very title, *Farewell to the Working Class* was bound to provoke hostility among Marxists dedicated to the class struggle. The subtitle of this book, *An Essay on Post-Industrial Socialism*, merely confirmed Gorz's outrageous absurdity – socialism without class struggle! If further confirmation of Gorz's heresy was needed, then one had to look no further than the titles of the first two chapters: 'The Working Class According to Saint Marx' and 'The Myth of Collective Appropriation'. Dogmatic Marxists could suspend their hatred for each other. At last they had a common enemy – Gorz. This is Gorz's only value for this dying breed.

However, the view that Gorz misrepresents Marx is one that is widely shared by more reasonable Marxists. We will thus take up this claim by pursuing the arguments advanced by Hyman. By focusing on Gorz's critique of Marx's theory of the proletariat, Hyman goes straight to the basis of the claim that Gorz misrepresents Marx. Gorz presents Marx's theory of the proletariat by paraphrasing *The Holy Family*, chapter 4, section IV. Here Marx writes,

> It is not a question of what this or that proletarian, or even the whole proletariat, at the moment *regards* as its aim. It is a question of *what the proletariat is*, and what, in accordance with this *being*, it will historically be compelled to do. Its aim and historical action is visibly and irrevocably foreshadowed in its own life situation as well as in the whole organisation of bourgeois society today.[16]

Statements such as this enable Gorz to argue that

> Marx's theory of the proletariat is not based upon either empirical observation of class conflict or practical involvement in proletarian struggle. No amount of empirical observation or practical involvement as a militant will lead to the discovery of the historical role of the proletariat – a role which, according to Marx, constitutes its being as a class. Marx made the point many times: empirical investigation of the real condition of the

proletariat will not disclose its class mission. On the contrary, only a knowledge of this mission will make it possible to discover the true being of the proletarians.[17]

Hyman takes exception to this. He echoes the sentiments of most Marxists when he states that 'Marx and Engels were surely profoundly influenced by their involvement with the empirical working class ... Thus it is incorrect to regard Marx's theory as without empirical foundation.'[18] Of course Marx and Engels 'were profoundly influenced by their involvement with the empirical working class'. This is *not* what Gorz is saying. Hyman misses the essential point, namely that Marx's theory of the proletariat is just that – theory. But more importantly it is a *theory that does not require empirical verification*. 'For the young Marx it was not the existence of a revolutionary proletariat that justified his theory. Instead his theory enabled him to predict the *inevitable* emergence of the revolutionary proletariat.'[19] Gorz adds:

> The analysis was governed by philosophy. Philosophy anticipated real developments: it demonstrated that the meaning of history lay in the emergence, with the proletariat, of a universal class alone able to emancipate society as a whole. This class *had to* emerge if history was to be meaningful, and *indeed there were already signs of the process taking place*.[20]

What is odd is that Hyman uses the same argument that Gorz does. He notes that Marx and Engels's 'vision of the proletariat was refracted by their philosophical polemic with the young Hegelians'.[21] Even though Hyman has it that Marx *'philosophically discovers the proletariat as agent of world revolution ... only after* moving to Paris in the autumn of 1843 and experiencing a working class which "pulsed with all the political and social movements ... "',[22] he does, as we have highlighted, admit that the proletariat was a philosophical discovery. To reinforce this interpretation Hyman could be embellishing Gorz when he writes:

> What *can* plausibly be argued is that the time and place in which Marx and Engels encountered the working class were exceptional; and that they were encouraged to treat the militant socialist worker as prototypical *because the stereotype meshed so neatly with their unfolding world-historical analysis*.[23]

In the very next sentence Hyman and Gorz become one. 'The extrapolation of the struggles of the 1840s into proletarian revolution,' Hyman tells us, *'was an act of faith*.'[24] Exactly. As Gorz maintains, 'The philosophy of the proletariat is a religion.'[25] Thus it is true that 'orthodoxy, dogmatism and religiosity are not therefore accidental features of marxism'.[26] And Hyman reinforces his 'conversion' to Gorz's interpretation in stating that 'it is not unreasonable to maintain *that faith became increasingly blind* when, despite the collapse of the upsurge of 1848, the grave-digging inevitably of victory was so confidently reiterated'.[27] To his credit Hyman realises that Gorz has not misrepresented Marx after all. 'Gorz quite rightly argues that this conviction has involved a mythological proletarian ideal; and that the failure of the empirical working class to conform to the prescribed model has encouraged all manner of substitutionist tendencies and projects.'[28] One–nil to Gorz.

Hyman does not let matters rest here. He takes up another tack. Against scientific Marxism he argues that 'Marxism also contains a divergent conception, in which workers' common class identity and political insurgency are not a mechanical outcome of material necessity'. He elaborates:

> The long *practical* involvement of Marx and Engels in the international working-class movement reflected a *contingent* theory of revolution: a task to be actively accomplished, not passively awaited. Marx does not 'guarantee the success of the revolution in advance or take it for granted. He only indicates its possibilities historically'.[29]

To support this claim, as if it needs supporting, Hyman identifies a number of 'distinct sources of Marx's identification of the working class as agent of revolution'. He states that 'they cannot be dismissed as cavalierly as Gorz imagines'.[30] The implication here is that Gorz misrepresents Marx by failing to give sufficient attention to Marx's alternative theory of revolution. Nothing could be further from the truth. Gorz, arguably more than any other living theorist, is a *representative* of this 'divergent conception' of revolution.

> Taking power implies taking it away from its holders, not by occupying their posts but by making it permanently impossible for them to keep their machinery of domination running. Revolution is first and foremost the irreversible destruction of this machinery. It implies a form of collective practice capable of bypassing and superseding it through the development of an alternative network of relations.[31]

Further, Gorz, apart from being a representative of an active theory of revolution, actually addresses certain of the forms that this theory takes.[32] More importantly, as a living representative of a living Marxism, Gorz's analysis of changes within capitalism demonstrates that the empirical sources of Marx's alternative theory of revolution, identified by Hyman, are no longer relevant.[33] Two–nil to Gorz.

But there are further scores to settle. Hyman recognises a contradiction in Marx's depiction of proletarianisation in relation to the proletarian revolution.

> If capitalist production progressively degrades and disables the proletariat, reducing the worker to a 'crippled monstrosity', how can the worker then take the stage of history as a 'new-fangled man' who overturns capitalist relations of production and domination and ushers in a new social order?[34]

'Gorz's answer' to this question, Hyman tells us, 'is that Marx envisaged the reappearance of the artisan in the guise of the polytechnic worker in high-technology industry'. Hyman then adds that 'this is surely a perverse reading of Marx'.[35] How can it be perverse? Gorz does provide textual support from Marx. Yet Hyman insists, in spite of this, that 'the thesis that advanced capitalism gave birth to a new category of polytechnic workers was not Marx's, but rather the enthusiasm of a number of left-wing French sociologists in the 1960s'.[36] In putting forward his answer to 'Marx's contradiction', Hyman falls back on his argument concerning the influence of proletarian activists on Marx. He admits that 'these "organic intellectuals"' were 'no doubt disproportionately drawn from an artisan stratum':[37] a clear own goal. Three–nil to Gorz.

So, Gorz's reading of Marx is not perverse after all. But with respect to 'the alternative thesis' in Marx, Hyman notes that it is 'one to which Gorz alludes'.[38] This is a gross understatement. Presumably Hyman thinks that 'alluding' is not good enough. This alternative thesis is spelled out by Hyman:

> Though the development of capitalist science and technology provides the material prerequisites for the emancipation of labour, by reducing necessary labour time and immensely increasing productivity, the actual consequences are not liberating but enslaving. The individual worker is no longer identifiably productive; established skills are eroded and displaced; the worker is subordinated to the machine; wages are depressed as women and children are employed in place of adult men; both the intensity and the length of the working day are increased.

At this point Hyman includes a lengthy passage from *Capital*, which he has drawn on above.[39] Hyman then argues that 'Marx assumed that workers were *bound* to rise up against such denial of their humanity'.[40] In other words Hyman has not identified an alternative thesis. He has merely restated Marx's metaphysical theory of the revolutionary proletariat.

This 'alternative thesis', Hyman adds, 'was never put to the test', because of the 'uneven character of proletarianisation', 'in other words against Gorz's thesis that full proletarianisation made revolutionary consciousness impossible'.[41] Hyman does not understand Gorz's argument. It was Marx's theory that demanded full proletarianisation. Gorz merely points out the logical consequences of this theory. Gorz himself does not believe full proletarianisation to be possible. Four–nil to Gorz.

There is in fact an alternative thesis in Marx. Gorz already identified this thesis in *Grundrisse* before he wrote *Farewell to the Working Class*. In *Strategy for Labour* Gorz includes a lengthy passage from *Grundrisse*.[42] This passage advances the argument that 'the measure of wealth is ... not labour time at all, but disposable time'.[43] It is an argument that appears throughout *Capital*. Gorz includes part of this passage in *Farewell to the Working Class*.[44] In this passage Marx approvingly cites from *The Source and Remedy*:

> Truly wealthy a nation, when the working day is 6 rather than 12 hours. *Wealth* is not command over surplus labour time [Marx adds, 'real wealth'], but rather, *disposable time* outside that needed in direct production, for *every individual* and the whole society.[45]

The alternative to revolution via proletarianisation in Marx is revolution by way of an active struggle to shorten the working day.[46] It is this alternative which has, with the publication of *Farewell to the Working Class* onwards, been taken up by Gorz as its foremost proponent. Five–nil to Gorz. In other words, no contest. Gorz knows his Marx better than Hyman does. Does anybody else fancy a game?

The concept of the neo-proletariat

Frankel, in claiming that Gorz believes the neo-proletariat to be 'the new revolutionary agent of change', reproduces a common misunderstanding.[47] For the record, 'the neo-proletariat' is 'a non-force, without objective social importance, excluded from society'.[48] It includes all those who can no longer identify with their work. Gorz provides empirical data in support of the view that:

> An inversion of the scale of priorities, involving a subordination of socialised work governed by the economy to activities constituting the sphere of individual autonomy, is underway in every class within the over-developed societies and particularly among the post-industrial proletariat. 'Real life' begins outside of work, and work itself has become a means towards the extension of the sphere of non-work, a temporary occupation by which individuals acquire the possibility of pursuing their main activities.[49]

Gorz goes on to stress that 'this is *a cultural mutation*'.[50] 'But it will only eliminate capitalism if its latent content is revealed in the form of an alternative to capitalism that is able to capture the developing cultural mutation and give it political extension.'[51] The neo-proletariat is 'the *possible* social subject of the struggle for work-sharing, generalised reduction of work time, gradual abolition of waged work ... and for a living income for all'.[52]

In the light of this clarification it also ought to be clear that the neo-proletariat cannot be thought of as only the unemployed and intermittently employed, as Hyman, among others, assumes. But, more significantly, Hyman questions the extent to which the cultural mutation actually exists. '"Gis-a-job" is not the cry of those who have abandoned the work ethic ... There is little evidence, either, that hierarchy and authority have lost their legitimacy in the eyes of the proletariat.'[53] Hyman's criticisms of Gorz here are entirely irrelevant. Wanting a job, more often than not, is wanting an income. It cannot be interpreted as an expression of the work ethic. Similarly, in an era of job insecurity, once in a job most workers will pragmatically defer to authority and appear to respect hierarchy. This cannot be taken to mean that they believe authority and hierarchy in the workplace to be legitimate. Paul Ransome is instructive on this point:

> It seems highly probable that the key reason why people continue to express such a strong willingness to participate in the labour process, stems more or less directly from the fact *that there is no practical alternative available to them*. Put bluntly, people remain willing to participate in the labour process because this is both seen to be, and for all immediate practical purposes actually is, *the only means by which they can gain access to necessary resources*.[54]

Heteronomy and autonomy in a future socialism

Gorz's model of a future socialist society, in which the sphere of heteronomy is subordinated to the sphere of autonomy, was originally introduced in *Farewell to the Working Class*. This model was presented in a chapter titled 'Towards a Dual Society'. This is not to be confused with 'the dual' society implied in Gorz's critique of the 'dualisation of society' which currently characterises the advanced capitalist societies. Since most of the critiques of Gorz's socialism refer to his model as one of 'a dual society', we shall follow this convention here, even though Gorz has stopped using the term.[55]

In the previous chapter we argued that the distinctiveness of Gorz's dual society can be grasped by contrasting it with the visions of socialism based on the collective ownership and control of the means of production on the one hand, and a welfarist model of socialism on the other. As we saw, Gorz's argument in support of his model is based on his critique of collective appropriation, informed by highly practical considerations of the consequences of the division of labour for workers' experience. Put crudely, efficient forms of production (its organisation and methods) inevitably involve workers experiencing alienation in heteronomous labour. This alienation, in practice, Gorz argues, cannot be eliminated by workers taking over the means of production. The 'workers' utopia' has it that the interests of the individual worker and the collective coincide. The worker is expected to identify with her or his work on the grounds that it contributes to the freedom of the whole society. In effect, given the complex and highly fragmented division of labour, the worker is required to identify with alienated work in the name of freedom. Of course, this is a nonsense. Socialism in this form denies the freedom of individual workers. Freedom would be best served, Gorz argues, not by glorifying alienated work, but by reducing our involvement in it. This can be achieved by making the production of necessities ever more efficient, enabling savings in labour time, which the whole society can share. Gorz argues that Marx anticipated this model. Marx wrote:

> In fact, the realm of freedom actually begins only where labour which is determined by necessity and mundane considerations ceases ... Freedom in this field ... [the realm of necessity] ... can only consist in socialised man, the associated producers, rationally regulating their interchange with Nature, bringing it under their common control ... and achieving this with the least expenditure of energy and under conditions most favourable to, and worthy of, their human nature. But it nonetheless remains a realm of necessity.

In other words, workers' control can, at best, deliver a limited freedom. Continuing the passage above, Marx states that:

> Beyond it ... [the realm of necessity] ... begins that development of human energy which is an end in itself, the true realm of freedom, which, however, can blossom forth only with this realm of necessity as its basis. The shortening of the working-day is its basic prerequisite.[56]

Gorz's model of socialism, then, distances itself from 'freedom within necessity', and reflects a commitment to 'freedom beyond necessity' – 'the true realm of freedom'. As such his model also distances itself from an altogether different conception of socialism – that based on a society made up of self-managed small communities. In fact Gorz offers a highly penetrative critique of this particular model. While the intent of the 'communalist' model to abolish heteronomous production is laudable enough,

> the realm of necessity is not abolished but sublimated, – and in this sublimated form – it continues to govern every moment of communal life: timetables, strict rules and obligations, hierarchy and discipline, division of tasks, the duty of obedience, devotion and love.[57]

Members of such communities have to pretend to freely choose their tasks and duties, and thus become agents of their own suffocation and self-denial. Again, Gorz's commitment to the development of 'the true realm of freedom' is abundantly clear, but echoing Marx, this development can happen only if we recognise necessity for what it is. Thus Gorz argues:

> Only a dissociation of the spheres of heteronomy and autonomy makes it possible to confine objective necessities and obligations to a clearly circumscribed area, and thus open up a space for autonomy entirely free of their imperatives. This is as true of large societies as of micro-societies based on communal life and production.[58]

Most of the criticisms of Gorz's dual society dwell on two aspects of the same issue. Gorz, it is claimed, exaggerates both the experienced alienation of heteronomous labour, and the lack of autonomy in the workplace. Sayers is not alone in stating that Gorz believes heteronomous work to be 'necessarily and ineliminably alienating'.[59] 'It is a mistake,' Sayers writes, 'to regard all forms of employment in a purely negative light.'[60] Similarly it is argued that Gorz's dual society is based on the impossible distinction between heteronomy and autonomy. Thus Hodgson observes that 'capitalist control of the labour process conflicts with limited but *necessary* worker autonomy in production'.[61]

There are two vital points to be made here. First, these 'criticisms' of Gorz are invalid because Gorz himself makes it perfectly clear that some autonomy is available in heteronomous labour, and that the latter may provide satisfactions which make it something less than total alienation.[62] Second, because these 'criticisms' are invalid – they merely state the obvious, which Gorz has already stated anyway – they cannot provide a basis for the rejection of Gorz's model of socialism. In fact these 'criticisms' fail to address the *principle* that the sphere of heteronomy should be made to serve autonomous projects and activities.

We get closer to criticisms of the principles and organisation of the dual society in the discussions offered by Giddens and Frankel. While Giddens provides a fair and accurate summary of *Farewell to the Working Class*, in which he acknowledges that 'the two sectors in the dual society ... will not be entirely separate from one another',[63] he criticises Gorz's model on the grounds that it 'is more unrealistic and naive than the conceptions of democracy which he rejects'.[64] More unrealistic than workers' control or a society made up of self-managed communes? No. Giddens has something else in mind. In spite of Gorz's insistence that the dual society requires a state that embodies plans and policies which are democratically produced, Giddens accuses Gorz of having a 'dismissive attitude towards economic and political democracy'. He then patronisingly offers Gorz a sociology lesson.

> The 'state' is no longer a phenomenon clearly separable from 'civil society', and if there is one trend that does seem to move implacably forward, it is the expanding character of state involvement in even many of the minutiae of daily life.[65]

True, Gorz had made the same point ten years earlier.[66] But, Giddens continues, 'It is less plausible to suppose (as Gorz does, here coming in curious alignment with the contemporary Right) that this process can be reversed than it is to argue that its hierarchical, arbitrary, or impersonal aspects can be countered.'[67] It would be appropriate to suggest that it is Giddens who has a 'dismissive attitude towards economic and political democracy'. He is less concerned with democratically planned social transformation than he is with putting a 'democratic' gloss on existing institutions.[68]

Frankel, like Giddens, is both a critic and defender of 'welfare capitalism'. His book, *The Post-Industrial Utopians*, attempts to assess the work of Rudolf Bahro, Barry Jones, Alvin Toffler and Gorz in relation to his own proposals for a feasible post-industrial socialism.[69] Frankel's reading (or, more accurately, 'misreading') of Gorz is driven more by his own concerns than by a careful engagement with Gorz. Given that Frankel's book is littered with misrepresentations of Gorz, it will be of little value to the Gorz scholar. Unlike Giddens's more accurate portrayal of the relation between the spheres of heteronomy and autonomy, Frankel repeats Berger and Kostede's 'criticism' that the division between the two spheres is too rigid.[70] Nonsensically, Frankel states that: 'The problem with Gorz is that he does not outline in detail how the sphere of autonomy will interact with the sphere of heteronomy (paid work, state regulation and planning, etc.).'[71] Quite what to 'outline in detail' means only Frankel knows.

Strangely, Frankel does refer to *Paths to Paradise*, yet somehow fails to acknowledge that a substantial part of this book does address the relationship between the two spheres. This kind of failure is frequently repeated throughout Frankel's book. He is forever criticising Gorz for what Gorz does not write about. This can be a useful critical ploy – if, for example, Gorz failed to address issues central to the validity and coherence of his project. However, Frankel's use of this ploy is invariably inappropriate. The 'absences' in Gorz's discussions either do not exist (they are, in fact, absences in Frankel's reading of Gorz), or they are acceptable. It is unreasonable to expect 'all the details' to be provided in the space of two short books. More than this, it is wrong to expect Gorz to spell out what, in Gorz's scheme, are to be the outcomes of democratic decision-making. A feature of Gorz's writings is his push towards an emancipatory future. He writes about 'what is possible'. Of course, Gorz has his own preferences, and he does develop proposals for the future. But his own proposals are not blueprints – they illustrate what is possible. And, importantly, they cannot be blueprints for the simple reason that the essential element of Gorz's future socialism is that we must make it for ourselves, *democratically*.

A reasonable question to ask about Gorz's dual society is: what will happen to existing welfare arrangements? Gorz does provide some answers. But, as usual, Frankel wants more from Gorz. He states that the division between the spheres of heteronomy and autonomy

> is far from satisfactory when it comes to alternatives to existing social welfare services. The reason for this is that Gorz has failed to spell out the nature of housework, childcare, care for the aged, sick, etc., and in what way these tasks will be part of either autonomous or heteronomous spheres.[72]

It was not until the publication of *Critique of Economic Reason* that Gorz addressed these issues in detail.[73] Even so, Gorz had already said enough in *Farewell to the Working Class* for Rojek to mistakenly conclude that Gorz's dual society embodied a full-blown welfare state. Sayers is equally mistaken in drawing the opposite conclusion, namely that Gorz, in keeping with right-wing policies, advocates the dismantling of the welfare state.[74] For the record, Gorz is no ally of the Right. He describes the Right's 'condemnation of the welfare state in the name of economic liberalism' as 'a piece of mindless ideology'. He continues:

> State provision does not stifle society and limit the spontaneous deployment of economic rationality; it is born of this very deployment, as a substitute for the societal and familial solidarity that the extension of commodity relations has dissolved, and as a necessary framework preventing the market economy finishing up in a collective disaster.[75]

Furthermore, 'it is not a question of dismantling the welfare state but of relieving it'.[76] The expansion of the sphere of autonomy 'may *give rise* to a limited reduction in the service and provision requirements of the welfare state'.

> In other words, when free time ceases to be scarce, certain educative, caring and assistance activities and the like may be partially repatriated into the sphere of autonomous activities and reduce the demand for these things to be provided by external services, whether public or commercial.[77]

'*When free time ceases to be scarce*' is the crucial factor which radically separates Gorz's proposals from those of the Right. And, this is what Sayers fails to grasp. Gorz insists that:

> An expansion in the sphere of autonomous activities cannot, by definition, *come about as a result of* a policy which reduces state provision and state services, thus leaving those social strata least able to do so to fend for themselves. The expansion of a sphere of autonomy always presupposes that, time no longer being counted, individuals have chosen to repatriate into the domestic or microsocial sphere of voluntary co-operation activities which, for want of time, they had abandoned to external services.[78]

Repatriating activities to the domestic sphere is a part of Gorz's proposals to relieve the welfare state in a future socialist society. But, it is just this, some have argued, that makes Gorz 'reactionary and misguided'.[79] It would seem, in the eyes of some critics, that Gorz's dual society will return us to the traditions of the domestic confinement of women.

Gorz's alleged sexism

We have just noted one reason why the likes of Sayers and Frankel suspect Gorz, if not of blatant sexism, at least of 'gender-blindness' and of collaboration with patriarchy. If we add to this Gorz's critique of wages for housework proposals, and his critique of socialised domestic labour, the politically correct feminist sympathiser has no option but to condemn Gorz as a sexist. If confirmation of this condemnation is required then one need look no further than Gorz's discussion of prostitution.[80]

Gorz's problem, as far as Hyman sees it, is that he is unfamiliar with the literature of British and American feminism.[81] Significantly, Hyman does not mention one text that Gorz should read. Perhaps it is Gorz's ignorance of feminism which has led him to neglect 'the international economic implications of gender discrimination and exploitation'.[82] Here, Frankel is carelessly repeating Illich's assessment of Gorz's argument about the impact of technology on the future of work. In actual fact, Illich regards Gorz's argument as 'brilliant'. He goes on to say, however, that Gorz's argument is '*mostly* blind to the issue of sex discrimination within this new international housework'.[83] Frankel takes this to mean that Gorz is neglectful of gender issues. He is mistaken. 'This new international housework', of which Illich speaks, *is not to be taken literally*. Illich is not referring to domestic labour as ordinarily understood.

> The majorities in underdeveloped nations increasingly assume a function that is *analogous* to the 'housewife' of the 'wage earner' [in the industrialised world]. Therefore, one can talk about what goes on at the periphery of industrial society as an international *Verhausfraulichung* [housewiferization].[84]

And, earlier, Illich asks if 'the Latin American slum dweller' is 'within the world economy, the new genderless housekeeper of the northern partner?'[85] Clearly, Illich is talking about the unemployed in the Third World. So much for Frankel's scholarship.

With respect to domestic labour proper, Gorz is fully aware of its role in the oppression of women, and does not propose that it should be a 'labour of love' in his dual society, as Sayers seems to think.[86] But if domestic labour is not a labour of love, 'If', as Frankel asks, 'these domestic tasks are servile (to use Gorz's term), then why should these "heteronomous" tasks not be paid for just like other forms of heteronomous labour?'[87]

As usual, Frankel has got things wrong. Domestic tasks are servile when they are heteronomously provided, and when they are performed in unequal households as a duty. Domestic labour does not have to be servile if it is performed equally, by equals, for each other. The 'emancipation of women' will have 'been finally achieved', Gorz argues, when 'man and woman voluntarily share the tasks of the private sphere *as well as those in the public sphere* and belong *equally* to one another'.[88] Our emphasis is made to drive home the point that it is futile to read Gorz's discussions on domestic labour and wages for housework as isolated discourses split off from his overall project. Gorz's proposals for reduced working hours benefiting the whole of society, in terms of extending employment opportunities to every adult, expanding the sphere of autonomy for everyone, and in terms of enabling everyone to have an income for life not only makes wages for housework redundant, but significantly contributes to the emancipation of women. This cannot be said of wages for housework policies.

Wages for housework, if such a policy was to be introduced, would tend 'to exclude women from work in the economic sphere' and would perpetuate 'the obligation for men to work full time'. As Gorz says, 'A fundamental choice about the kind of society we want to live in is involved here.'[89] All the more so, given that the level of payment for housework would reinforce the lowly status of domestic labour.

> Besides, the search for higher productivity would lead to the standardisation and industrialisation of such activities, particularly those involving the feeding, minding, raising and education of children. The last enclave of individual or communal autonomy would disappear; socialisation, 'commodification' and pre-programming would be extended to the last vestiges of self-determined and self-regulated life.[90]

In *Critique of Economic Reason*, Gorz develops this argument in considerable detail.[91] Bowring succinctly summarises the central theme:

> If work-for-oneself is regarded in terms of its social utility, efficiency and economic productivity, then there is no rational basis on which to resist society's claim to take charge of the most intimate and specific of human activities – including the socialisation of the reproduction of life – on the grounds of increased efficiency and according to the needs of the social system.[92]

There is clearly a warning in Gorz's writings that certain currents in feminism that argue for payment for housework and payment for motherhood on the grounds of social utility are collaborating, in theory at least, with a potentially suffocating totalitarianism – the opposite of liberation. Payment for motherhood on these grounds (social utility) would mean that 'the mother ... loses both her sovereign rights over her children and her rights over her own self'. Gorz continues:

> If she fails to fulfil the obligations society prescribes for her, she may be deprived of her rights as a mother. She is socialised and colonised to the depths of her very being and remains what patriarchal societies have always wanted her to be: a humble body which societies use for their own ends.
>
> A 'wage for motherhood' instituted in the name of 'the social usefulness of the maternal function' therefore introduces the idea that a woman may become the equivalent of a surrogate mother for society. The state may rent her womb in order to get its supply of children.[93]

Needless to say this 'plays right into the hands of the technocratic authoritarian spirit of domination'.[94]

Rather than telling Gorz to familiarise himself with feminist literature – much of which conforms to the stultifying pressures of political correctness – it might be suggested that some feminists acquaint themselves with Gorz's writings.

Gorz's alleged ethnocentrism

We have already noted Illich's view that Gorz is 'mostly blind' to the role of 'the Latin American slum dweller ... within the world economy'. The implication here is that Gorz can be criticised for ethnocentrism. Whatever awareness Gorz has of the plight of the unemployed in the Third World, Illich may be suggesting that this has not substantially influenced the arguments of *Farewell to the Working Class*. It is true that Gorz has very little to say about Third World peoples in this book. But this does not disqualify his analysis on the grounds of ethnocentrism.

It is somewhat surprising that Illich should have made this particular criticism of Gorz. Gorz, in different terminology to that created by Illich, not only revealed an awareness of Illich's 'new' international division of labour, at least as early as 1966, but saw both the impoverished in the Third World and in the affluent world as victims of 'colonialism'. 'Colonialism', Gorz argued, 'is not merely an *external* practice of modern capitalism, but also an *internal* practice going on within the imperialist country and extending without any break in continuity to countries beyond its frontiers.'[95]

> I think it is important to stress the fact that the dividing line between development and underdevelopment, dominating economic powers and dominated populations, colonisers and colonised, is one that runs not only *between* nations but also *within* every nation in the capitalist world.[96]

At the same time as Illich was writing *Gender*, Gorz was writing *Paths to Paradise*, in which he warned of the dualistic stratification of society. Gorz, in a manner akin to Illich, wrote:

> We are left ... with the sort of economy now predominant in parts of North and South America (New York, Brazil, Mexico, etc.) where pauperism and overabundance of commodity goods and services go hand in hand, where organised society marginalises and represses a dispossessed social majority: slum-dwellers in the shadows of skyscrapers precariously surviving on crime and the underground economy.[97]

Gorz's observations on the dualistic stratification of society continue to be an integral part of his analysis of social disintegration. In *Capitalism, Socialism, Ecology*, he refers to 'the dualisation of society' as 'a kind of South-Africanisation'.[98] Perhaps Illich would prefer it for Gorz to refer to 'a kind of Latin Americanisation'!

Are there other grounds for depicting Gorz's thinking as ethnocentric? Barry Smart seems to think that there are. He refers to Gorz's work in terms of its revealing 'aspects of' an 'overriding ethnocentric Western bias'.[99] In support of this claim Smart quotes Frankel of all people! Frankel states that 'it is difficult to accept that Gorz's concern with ecological goals and the abolition of imperialism in the Third World goes any deeper than a generalised moral critique of Western affluence and wasteful consumption'.[100] From our very brief discussion of Gorz's analysis of consumerism it is more than clear that Frankel is talking nonsense. Even more absurd is Smart's comment that 'it is hard to understand how the transformation proposed for ... [the industrialised capitalist countries] ... will effect any significant improvement in ... [the non-industrialised countries of the Southern Hemisphere]'.[101]

One does not have to read Gorz to achieve the understanding that escapes Smart – merely thinking through the consequences of lower levels of consumption in the affluent societies will do.

An issue related to Gorz's alleged ethnocentrism is that concerning the feasibility of Gorz's politics of time in the context of a growing internationalisation of capitalism. Smart draws on Keane and Owens who correctly state that

> the new international division of labour, changes in the global monetary and trading systems and super-power strategies would all loom large as obstructive factors in any single employment society's attempt to make a transition to socialism in Gorz's sense.[102]

Smart, however, repeats a common error when he notes that 'there is the implication in Gorz's work that a radical socioeconomic transformation might be achieved within a *national* context'.[103]

First, Gorz is in entire agreement with Keane and Owens's statement. Second – and this is Smart's error – it is precisely because of the power of international capital that Gorz proposes an *international* response. Smart lists *Paths to Paradise* in his bibliography, but appears not to have read Gorz's final section in which his internationalism is clear.[104] Further, in *Critique of Economic Reason*, which was published in English three years before the publication of Smart's book, Gorz refers to 'the regulatory power of nation states' having 'been overcome ... by the internationalisation of capital'. He points out that:

> Only a transnational Left coalition based on common political objectives could have resisted the internationalism of capital for any length of time. No such coalition emerged. The sole ambition of the majority of parties of the Left was to seize or retain control of the state apparatus. The members of the party machines thought in terms of positions of power within national power structures, without seeing that these national structures

were being emptied of all substance and decisions were now being taken elsewhere.[105]

And, when considering the conditions necessary for 'a rebirth of the Left', Gorz insists that 'the first of these conditions is internationalism'.[106] He then goes on to spell out precisely what this means.

Gorz's tendency to 'exaggerate' social changes

We have already noted that Gorz's critics have accused him of exaggerating the declining significance of work in people's lives, and the depth of alienation in the workplace. A related criticism is that advanced by Giddens in his critique of *Farewell to the Working Class*. Giddens concluded his critique by suggesting that 'the "high technology, low employment" society might turn out to be chimerical, itself the result of an over-generalization from certain trends of the moment'.[107]

So, did Gorz in *Farewell to the Working Class* over-generalize 'from certain trends of the moment'? Enough time has passed since the publication of the book for this question to be answered by way of reference to relevant empirical data. Ransome has in fact done just this. He has reproduced a wide range of official statistics which clearly indicate that the trends Gorz predicted have indeed become established features of the advanced capitalist societies.[108] Most of the statistics used by Ransome concern the United Kingdom between 1979 and 1989. During this period the workforce has grown, the number of 'economically active' people has increased, but at a rate which does not match the growth in unemployment. The increase in the number of economically active people is mostly accounted for by women in part-time employment. The most significant shifts in employment have seen a sharp decline in the percentage of the workforce in manufacturing industries, with an equivalent increase in the percentage of the workforce employed in the service sector. Furthermore these trends are reflected throughout the advanced capitalist societies in Europe.[109]

Most relevant to Gorz's predictions, Ransome notes that:

> With regard to effects on the distribution of employment, it is evident that many applications of microelectronic technology have induced shifts between different sectors of employment, and, in some cases, have dramatically reduced the quantity of labour required to produce the same or greater output than was possible prior to their introduction. Perhaps the clearest illustrations of this latter trend have emerged in coalmining and vehicles manufacture where advanced technology systems and flexible specialisation have greatly improved output whilst directly reducing employment.[110]

All of the trends noted above, Ransome maintains, 'are relatively permanent rather than transitory changes'.[111] More recently, with respect to the economies of the advanced industrialised societies, Ransome concludes that 'there is no question that these economies have entered an important period of transition, and that the momentum for change is now too firmly established to be disregarded as simply a temporary phenomenon'.[112]

As micro-electronic technology spreads to the service sector, we find that the expansion of employment in, for example, banking, finance and insurance, which occurred between 1979 and 1989, has not only been halted, but reversed.[113] In his diligent monitoring of employment statistics since 1990, Bowring provides ample evidence that new forms of technology are 'rapidly reducing the amount of both labour and capital required to produce an expanding volume of production'.[114]

A major social consequence of changing patterns of employment is the dual stratification of society. By 1993, only 35.9 per cent of the workforce in the UK were in secure, full-time employment.[115] And, according to Will Hutton's calculations, 29 per cent of the working population, by 1995, were made up of the economically inactive, the unemployed, and those on government training schemes.[116]

Are all of these trends connected to the cultural changes of which Gorz speaks? Has Gorz exaggerated the extent to which a majority of the working population are distancing themselves from work? Smart, for one, believes that Gorz exaggerates the willingness of people to work shorter hours for less pay. As he puts it, '"Work less, live more" is a very appealing slogan, but its attractiveness is diminished by the corollary "consume less"!'[117] In arguing that Gorz has underestimated the strength of consumer motivations, Smart has failed to grasp the ways in which consumerism is manipulated, and ignores the growing evidence in support of Gorz's claim.[118]

Yet given the ways in which the academic world approaches consumerism, it can be anticipated that Smart will not be alone in identifying 'the desire to consume' as a major obstacle to a future socialism along the lines proposed by Gorz. Since this issue is of direct relevance to Gorz's political strategy, we will discuss it below.

Gorz's political strategy

There are two common criticisms of Gorz's political strategy. The first is addressed to the lack of a political strategy in *Farewell to the Working Class*. Even though Gorz states that 'I have ... deliberately left this question (that is, the question of political strategy) open and unresolved',[119] Hyman sees fit to exploit this 'absence'. He argues that Gorz fails to confront 'the problems inherent in a socialist challenge to the mechanisms and vested interests of class rule'; that 'Gorz seemingly proposes that socialism will be established through spiritual conversion alone'; and that 'Gorz is very imprecise in locating the *agency* of socialist advance'.[120]

The criticism concerning the difficulties facing the development of socialism is a surprising one. Gorz addressed these problems in some detail in *Strategy for Labour*, and in *Socialism and Revolution*. Further, Gorz has never proposed 'spiritual conversion' as the means of establishing socialism. This 'criticism' together with that of Gorz's failure to identify the 'agency of socialist advance' have become redundant in the light of Gorz's writings since *Farewell to the Working Class*.

The second common criticism of Gorz's political strategy, as we have already noted, revolves around Gorz's alleged failure to appreciate the significance of consumerism as an obstacle to the kind of socialism he advocates. This criticism is voiced by Smart:

> The fact that a majority of the population in Western industrial capitalist societies seems to be imbued with an increasing desire to consume, that their very identities may be synonymous with their status as consumer subjects, raises serious questions about the prospects and possibilities for a radical transformation of the social system in the direction advocated by Gorz.[121]

It is fair to say that the kind of criticism made by Smart will find considerable support, not only among sociologists of culture, but also among certain sections of the left.[122] The pleasures derived from consumerism are, it is widely argued, so firmly established within the affluent societies, that people will be unwilling to give them up lightly. These pleasures, it is further argued, are hardened by the value (symbolic value) of consumer goods and services for contemporary identity-construction. Needless to say these arguments suggest that any politics involving reduced levels of consumption will meet resistance from a majority.

The superficiality of these arguments can be revealed by a brief consideration of the standard sociological approaches to consumer culture, as presented by Mike Featherstone. He discusses three of the major sociological perspectives on consumer culture. Two of these perspectives have been alluded to by Smart – the use of goods for identity-formation, and the focus on consumption as a source of pleasure. In keeping with sociological trends, Featherstone argues that these two approaches are important correctives to the third approach, which he refers to as 'the production of consumption' perspective. Gorz is the main contemporary representative of 'the production of consumption' perspective, though Featherstone believes that it has been best developed in the writings of the Frankfurt School and Henri Lefebvre.[123] According to Featherstone, one should 'not merely regard consumption as derived unproblematically from production' but should also consider the symbolic value of consumer goods for identity formation, and the 'emotional pleasures of consumption' in explaining consumer activity.[124] Of course, neither the Frankfurt School, nor Gorz, 'regard consumption as derived unproblematically from production'. We will return to Featherstone's misunderstanding shortly.

There is no doubt that some consumer activity can be explained in terms of anticipated pleasures. It would be foolish, however, to ignore the fact that there is something that might be called 'necessary consumption', that is consumption driven by need. Again, it is safe to assume that some pleasure may be derived from the satisfaction of need. But part and parcel of the definition of consumerism, or consumer culture is that it is a post-necessity phenomenon. In other words, the motivations underpinning consumerism are not needs-based. As such they are nowhere near as powerful as the likes of Featherstone and Smart assume. This fact is corroborated in a number of surveys.[125]

It is significant, too, that when addressing the question of consumerism and identity, Featherstone ignores identity-needs. Rather the focus is on 'the different ways in which people use goods in order to create' superficial 'social bonds or distinctions'.[126] In other words identity is treated as a surface display of association and difference, expressing lifestyle preferences. We can readily recognise that goods and services are used in this way. But the relevance of superficial displays of identity for the need for a satisfying sense of self must be seriously doubted.[127] We can say that people's 'identities may be synonymous with their status as consumer subjects' *only if* we adopt a trivial concept of identity.

Positing consumerism as an obstacle to progressive social change arises from a disregard for how the majority experience consumerism. At a theoretical level it arises from a failure to understand the ways in which the Frankfurt School and Gorz depict consumption as a consequence of the stranglehold the capitalist system exercises over the satisfaction of experienced needs.[128] Of vital importance – and this escapes Featherstone's orthodoxy – is Gorz's argument that high levels of consumption are directly related to inflated working hours, which themselves are, in part, the consequence of superfluous production. It is not consumerism that is an obstacle to Gorz's socialism, rather, the obstacles are embodied within the system, including its relations of domination and subordination, which generates and maintains consumerism.

Conclusions

It must be noted that in presenting criticisms of Gorz, we have not attempted to voice the more approving comments of his critics. Many of the critics we have referred to do concede that there is much of value in Gorz's writings. Hyman, for example, elaborates in some detail on his view that 'Gorz's discussion of the interrelationship between state, socialism and individualism is of urgent import'. Some of Gorz's arguments in this regard, Hyman finds 'wholly persuasive'.[129]

An inevitable consequence of our focus on *criticisms* of Gorz is that the reader may be left with the impression that the whole world is against Gorz. This is far from the case. Apart from major intellectuals of the past, such as Sartre and Marcuse, acknowledging Gorz's significant contribution to socialism,[130] some of today's most influential thinkers have either drawn on Gorz or praised his writings. Habermas, for example, uses Gorz to advance his own critique of right-wing ideology.[131] And, in spite of the controversy surrounding *Farewell to the Working Class*, Claus Offe refers to it as a 'marvellous book'.[132] In fact, it is fair to say that Gorz has been highly influential for almost 40 years. *La Morale de l'histoire* became a subversive Marxist text in Italy, Mexico and Spain, but it was not until the publication of *Strategy for Labour* in 1967 that Gorz began to attract a loyal following in the English-speaking world. Bob Connell, for example, described *Strategy for Labour* as 'paradigmatic' in terms of articulating a 'renewed concern among socialist theorists with the practical problems of labour movements'.[133] Connell praises Gorz for taking 'the trouble to make a close, historically concrete, study of what various groups of workers actually *do* in their daily lives'.[134]

While Gorz has reformulated his strategy for the labour movement, he has nevertheless remained highly sensitive to the lived experience of workers, whether full-time or intermittent. It is not surprising, therefore, that his writings have been described as the 'clearest link between politics, practice and theory'.[135] As such his influence has been wide-ranging – informing critiques of work,[136] the future of employment,[137] and attempts to formulate a feasible socialism.[138] He also has his supporters among those of a Green persuasion.[139]

Overall, we have much sympathy with Bowring's displeasure at 'the poor reception of his [Gorz's] ideas in Britain'. This 'stands in stark contrast to the popularity of Gorz's work on the Continent, where in many countries the issue of reduced working hours is firmly on the political agenda as a means for tackling unemployment'.[140] In defence of his critics, we can say that some of them at least have read Gorz, albeit carelessly. What is far more noticeable, however, is the extent to which Gorz is ignored. Bowring notes the widespread neglect of Gorz's work in debates on economic democracy, market socialism, the labour process and latest forms of work. But 'what is most striking is the reluctance of British commentators to consider Gorz's proposals for reducing working time and guaranteeing an income independent of the number of hours worked'. Bowring goes on to express dismay at the failure of one of our more enlightened publications to make a single reference to Gorz in their collection of essays on the need for time.[141]

The neglect of Gorz is not restricted to areas of debate where one might most expect Gorz's work to be crucial. Bowring mentions the importance of Gorz's critique of 'the sociologistic conception of the lifeworld', of his 'phenomenological interpretation of the political ecology movement', and of his 'persuasive argument against wages for housework'. Bowring concludes his excellent paper on the reception of Gorz by stating that: 'It is frustrating to be misunderstood, but an insult to be ignored. A more faithful reading of Gorz will prove the relevance of his work to the problems of today.'[142]

Gorz's relevance is assured because he takes his cues, not from academic fashion, but from the lived experience of the majority. This is essential for critical social theory and the socialist movement. Gorz's continuing critique of the changing impact of capitalism on our lives, of the manipulation of needs and the distortion of our need for autonomy, of work and consumerism not only stands in sharp contrast to the superficialities generated by academic fashion, but provides the socialist movement with an avenue for reconnecting itself with 'ordinary' people. More than this, Gorz offers us a vision of a better future and practical ways of getting there. Gorz is one of the very few who has continued to maintain the unity of experience, theory and practice. At a time when social theory is becoming increasingly divorced from lived experience, and is losing its critical edge, and when the left is in dire need of rejuvenation, it does not make sense to ignore Gorz.

A Dialogue with Gorz

Jeremy Tatman: In *The Traitor* you state that in 1947 you believed Paris to be the centre of the world; the centre of truth. It is quite clear that the work of Jean-Paul Sartre, his circle and the whole intellectual climate at that time had a tremendous impact upon you. What was it that so excited you about Sartre's philosophical perspective, in contrast to traditional and alternative philosophical discourses at that time?[1]

André Gorz: To be honest, I did not know any other philosophy than Sartre. I had read a few philosophical books in the past, which I had not found very fascinating. However, with Sartre, after I had dug in for a few months, I found that it corresponded to what I was experiencing; which was to be completely illegitimate, unjustifiable, contingent in the philosophical sense of the word, condemned to self-determination ... It gave me the keys to interpret myself and to interpret the world, and I found these keys satisfactory. It was a philosophy of radical freedom, in search of authenticity; a denunciation of all the forms of bad faith, of seriousness, of conformism. It made you feel that a human being could build him- or herself.

JT: And why did you feel that this was important at that particular time?

AG: I was a half-Jew born in Austria who had lost his motherland; who was neither German, nor Jewish, nor anything else – who had no identity by birth, whose mother was in conflict with his father and whose father insisted that his mother was something very different from what he had expected. Who was living in a third country, Switzerland, where he certainly didn't fit in. The problem was knowing that he did not belong anywhere, and had no identity whatsoever on which he could rely, no role which he was expected to hold. How could I go on living? That was my problem.

JT: And yet in *The Traitor* you say that by 1946 everything seemed possible because people felt that they were making a new start. That after seven years in which the old forms had burst open and

117

intellectual activity had lost all sense of a subject, thinking assumed a terribly important status. In what ways had the experiences of the previous seven years made earlier philosophical discourses appear redundant or inapplicable to that reality?

AG: That is not exactly how it was. In 1945–6 in France – as well as in Italy, and as well as in Spain in 1976 – you had to catch up with all that you had forgotten in the previous six years. Which is that there is a critical thought, that there is something called Marxism, psychoanalysis – the Frankfurt School were also emerging at this time …

In America it was certainly different, as it was in Sweden, and in Britain too. There was no break of continuity in Britain. It came out of the Second World War as the same nation, certain of its rights, the cohesion of its society and its ideological base. The British were even capable of developing, without any break in continuity, the Beveridge Plan, social reform and the welfare system, and so on. It was an evolution, society having taken consciousness of itself and taking confidence in its capability to run itself – that was Britain then.

France, on the contrary, had to justify that France still existed, after all that it had done and not done as an occupied country collaborating with the enemy. And when you have to re-legitimate your existence as a nation, well, thinking takes on a tremendous importance. Also social thinking, of course, since the form of power that the bourgeoisie had in France before the war was the exact cause of its collapse during the war and of its acceptance of German occupation. It had to find itself another ruling class, or another class capable of ruling.

JT: The ideal, whereby individuals are able to move smoothly between different levels of existence without having to be subordinate to any of them, clearly informed your work of the 1940s and early 1950s. I would like to ask you the extent to which this is presently the case? I am thinking here of your proposals for a guaranteed income for life, your politics of time and the desire to eliminate all forms of oppression.

AG: Interesting question. It is the essence of modernity to differentiate different levels, neither of which is subordinated to the other. They each have their autonomy. A politics of time is precisely one that 'unlinks' the realm of socially necessary work from the realm of self-achievement, and from the realms of aesthetic pleasures and private intimacy. It refuses to have people specialise in any one of them. There should be no slaves specialising in socially necessary labour while others specialise in creative arts and so forth. Every person is entitled to move on all levels and have all the forms of life that they can have at the same time.

JT: You have always maintained that freedom is the only possible morality. How did you arrive at this conclusion and what are its implications?

AG: This is pure Sartre. You must start from the fact that human beings are free in whatever they do. Even their denial of being free is an act of freedom, but it is an act of self-denial at the same time. As long as you deny or refuse that you are free, which is the essence of bad faith, you are going to be very unhappy because your freedom is going to force itself upon you from behind. In this situation, you suffer your freedom. You cannot be what you want to be, which is someone who is identical with his role, his nation or his family or hierarchical position. You can never identify with what you want. You are doomed to be free. So the only way to be happy with it is to choose to be what you are.

But this is a break with the normal attitude, because socialisation, all socialisation, consists in hiding from the subjects that they are the subjects of their actions – that is the essence of socialisation. Society produces the social individual in such a way as to hide from him or her the fact that they are a subject. Education plays a great role in this process, unless it is an emancipatory form of education, which is not very widespread nowadays.

JT: While we are free beings, to what extent does this concept of human beings recognise social and material constraints upon our actions? For example, there are many people who are alienated within their work, and yet many of them may feel that they actually have little choice but to continue within it.

AG: An individual may experience their job as unsatisfactory because they are a free being; a being who aspires to a type of activity in which it realises itself and produces itself as being self, being an 'I'. When this possibility is taken away, a job will be experienced as alienating. You have to be someone else, you have to behave in a way that hides the fact that you feel what you feel, you are what you are and want what you want – that's alienation. Most people, in fact, when they can't change their working conditions, come to accept it and say afterwards: 'it's not that bad'. If they don't, they are already potentially radicalised.

JT: It is clear that you still consider *Fondements pour une morale* to be quite an original and effective account of the subjective reality of alienation. However, in *The Traitor* one gets the impression that at this time you were disillusioned with this work. Indeed, you refer to it as 'a sterile evasion', 'a means of escaping yourself' and 'an imitation' (of Sartre). Upon this basis you go on to state that a philosopher cannot dispense with life and that everything had to be started over again.

You seem to be implying that *Fondements pour une morale* was too abstract and that your philosophy and your very being had to be embellished with greater reference to your own subjective experience. Is it in this sense that you regard *The Traitor* as a practical application of its predecessor: that you began to *live* your theoretical postulates and attempt to realise an existential conversion of your own?

AG: Excellent question. There is a lot in that question ... I had been working on *Fondements pour une morale* for about nine years and I had a practical certainty that it would not be published. So what was my option? As they say in America, 'Get on with your life', invest yourself in something different, rather than suffering feelings of failure and losing all confidence in your capacity of doing anything. So I started with self-criticism, withdrawing from that piece ...

JT: Wasn't that also a way of pre-empting criticism? Wasn't it also the fact that you were awaiting Sartre's response to it? That's the impression that I got from the first chapter of *The Traitor*.

AG: I had no idea of what his response would be, but I certainly doubted that he would read it all. He was a very nice man, but he referred to the first page only ... My response was to withdraw from the book, because it could not lead me any further, and start something new. *Fondements pour une morale* was not only a theoretical construction, it was also a method for self-conversion. It worked out what questions to ask yourself, what self-analysis to undertake and what questions to ask about the empirical world around you in order to be capable of emancipating yourself from what you have been made by previous circumstances, and re-determine yourself in relation to what you feel that you validly want to be doing.

That's only the method, and the book itself was certainly not an implementation of that method. The method was implemented in *The Traitor*.

JT: In *Fondements pour une morale* your concern was the alienation of 'man in general' and the attempt to provide a basis towards its transcendence ...

AG: Fundamentally, *Fondements pour une morale* was an attempt to define and establish a hierarchy of values. The question is what values you are experiencing and why, and is there a hierarchical order between them? More than two-thirds of the book is about that.

JT: Is it possible, given your subjective feelings, interests and background at that time, to have established a method for 'man in general'? Do you think that such an approach is valid?

AG: Yes, definitely. There is a level of reflection on which every man can write true things about the constitution of man in general. The most basic level being, of course, that of sensory experience. There are things that are pleasurable or painful to any man – bodily experiments, pleasurable, voluptuous, beautiful – that is where I started. I started with sensory experience and moved on to aesthetic experience ... What is the essence of beauty? Why are certain things, landscapes for instance, beautiful and others are not? So all of this is, in my opinion, valid at all times. What is not, of course, is action, which is always relative to situations. But if there are situations that are more acceptable or less acceptable than others, the reason is in man himself – it is not in the situation. Some situations forbid, while others allow or even enhance the possibility of unfolding your sensory experience according to your bodily needs, to the essence of aesthetic aspirations, and to not have to subordinate your aspirations of self-determination and autonomy to considerations of necessity, opportunity and so on. So there are alienating situations and others that are not. The question is how can we produce a world in which there are no alienating situations, if that is a possibility. Anyway, you should be able to establish the prerequisites, and that was all that I was doing in the latter part of the book.

JT: Rather modestly, in the 'Afterword' to *The Traitor* you describe yourself as 'a failed philosopher, trying to smuggle in your original philosophical reflections through ostensibly political or sociological themes'. However, your work as a journalist and critical theorist has been more concerned with focusing upon and intervening in events in the empirical world – in particular, the way that it prevents freedom from being used creatively, towards its own self-realisation. Is it therefore the case that rather than being a 'failed philosopher' – after all, your aim was not to construct an abstract theoretical system – you have been more concerned to engage with contemporary events in the hope of encouraging people to question the meaning, purpose and value of their lives?

AG: Beautiful! What's the question? That is a statement. Thank you ... One thing that I should add is that that interview was done in 1983, when my latest book was *Farewell to the Working Class*. Since then I have written *Paths to Paradise*, which is already more philosophical that the previous one in certain respects and then I have written *Critique of Economic Reason*. After I had retired from journalism I was capable of producing a book which included all that I had learned: the radical social critique, my existential views on how the levels of existence are hierarchically ordered, and my first and most lasting interest, phenomenological analysis or reflection of self-experience, which is the part on the typology of working activities. *Critique of Economic Reason* has since been recognised as being a philosophical book.

JT: As you have just stated, *Critique of Economic Reason* is a more sophisticated book in terms of its depth and range of issues. Your retirement aside, what other factors encouraged you to write this particular text at this time?

AG: I started *Critique of Economic Reason* after I had written a number of articles covering many of the themes included in it. I then attempted to build it into a more coherent discourse. I started with the history of work as an invention of capitalism and at the same time I was reading Habermas's *Theory of Communicative Action*. Although Habermas was not especially interested in what I was interested in, I found themes, quotations and so forth which helped me to take new angles: what is the whole issue of modernity? ... Max Weber – the question of needs, of 'enough is enough' and 'more is more' grows out of Max Weber.

   The definition of the lifeworld also bothered me very much. There is a sort of philosophical and sociological contempt of the way that people *experience their life*, because calling the lifeworld all the habits and laws that you inherit from your ancestors and find normal, familiar, and therefore stick to, does not answer the question: '*How do you experience them?*' ... Muslim women who live in total oppression, who are circumcised in most of Africa, that is their lifeworld. They stick to it, but it doesn't tell you anything about their *quality* of life, their experience of it. There is an absence of the notion that there is a *quality* of living, of experiencing that lifeworld. The quality of this experience is the foundation of the critique of the lifeworld, which is never talked about in Habermas or the others who use that notion.

JT: In *The Traitor* you state that the child derives from its socio-cultural heritage the only project that he or she can be: 'a vital, subsequently religious project aiming at vital, subsequently mystical satisfactions'. Furthermore, you state that it is more difficult for those who are unable to recognise through their work that they make the world to liquidate the complexes and religious values of childhood. How do you perceive the development of 'mega-technologies' in this respect?

AG: People who never experience that they are producing themselves and the world have no leverage to reject the roles that they have been socialised into in childhood. This does not mean that this incapacity is enhanced by mega-technologies, because outside of the world of technologies you can gain lots of experiences which can help you to move out of these primary childhood experiences. That's the interesting thing. Nowadays people are not socialised primarily through their work, which may be experienced as totally alienating to them, as cogs in a big machine. They are socialised completely differently, through communicative relations with their own age group. For example, they socialise themselves against the school at school.

JT: I believe that you have already gone some way to answering my next question. In your earlier writings you felt that it was desirable, if people were to transcend their complexes, for them to recognise that they were producing themselves and their world within their work. However, following *Farewell to the Working Class* in 1980, you see the potential for social change only being realised with the support of precisely those people who *cannot* identify with their work. This represents a significant theoretical shift. How do you account for this?

AG: Following on from what I have just said, we have to ask ourselves why these people find themselves incapable of identifying with their work. It's mainly because work does not correspond to their deepest aspirations of self-fulfilment. The norm is different. The norm informing the critique of work is really a norm of autonomy. There are a number of books that have been published in Germany on the new cultural model and on the generational break between the people under 30 years of age and their parents. They are no longer prepared to sacrifice themselves for professional success. Even managerial workers prefer the life that they determine for themselves outside of work, as this is the realm in which they can attempt to achieve existential fulfilment. Similarly in France, a recent book which draws extensively upon opinion polls points to what it calls 'the cultural revolution of free time'.

JT: If this is now the case, why did you place so much emphasis upon the ability of people to recognise and produce themselves within their work in the past?

AG: Well, because the essential characteristic of a subject is that he or she produces him- or herself. A free, autonomous being is a being that is not determined by circumstances independent of its will, but one which uses circumstances to produce itself in a way that it can adhere to. I was, and still am to a certain extent, a Marxist. Work is *the* activity by which human beings produce the world and themselves. The fact is that they can't do that any longer in their professional life, because of mega-technologies, alienation, the abstraction of work and all that. It means that work in that sense has disappeared.

JT: Hence the need to provide resources, such as communal, convivial tools and greater free time, to enable people to fulfil themselves outside of the realm of necessity?

AG: Outside of the realm of their professional labour, yes, *which anyway takes less and less time in people's lives.*

JT: Was it through your contact with social reality in your professional life that Marxism became important to you? I know that the intellectual debates of the period were influential in this respect, particularly between Sartre and the Marxists, but can the same be said of investigating real-life situations as a journalist?

AG: I read Marx, although not very systematically, because I was looking for keys to interpret things that were going on. In France at that time we had got state planning, some top economists in all government positions, and it was important to first understand economics in order to be able to criticise what was going on and to understand class relations. I needed Marx just in my journalistic work and not the other way around.

JT: How do you assess the influence of May 1968 upon your work? I know that Adrian Little has suggested, in a paper that you have read, that it encouraged a more revisionist approach, including a search for a new motor of history based upon new social movements.[2] In this respect your concern with ecological issues and the movements based around them did come to feature prominently in your work. However, it was 1975 before *Ecologie et politique* was published.

AG: The real change that May 1968 has made only became obvious in the 1970s. It was a cultural revolt which made quite evident the change in values that had occurred in younger people, and the impossibility of continuing with politics and society as had been done up to that point. The left and socialism needed to be basically redefined.

After 1968, came this long period in which France, Italy and, to a certain extent, Germany became ungovernable. There was no longer any possibility of controlling strikes, of controlling the labour movement – not even the unions could control it. It was as though the workers had decided that they were as good as the students in taking powers wherever they were and to make the places of work into places of living. To me, the real revolution of 1968 was that. So up to 1973, as you can see in *The Division of Labour*, I was writing mainly about the possibility of turning places of production into places of self-determination, self-production, the production of society and the production of democracy. And, as you know, it took me some time before I discovered that the division of labour was not just a specialisation beginning in the place of production; it was over whole continents, it was a spatial division of labour, not just a professional one.

JT: And therefore work increasingly became opaque …

AG: And therefore people had no idea of what they were doing, they had no control over production … power was located elsewhere. Ecology was for me a revolution under a different form and from a different angle. Since you cannot revolutionise society from the angle of reappropriating industrial work, political ecology was the one angle through which you could show that the capitalist system cannot survive unless it totally subverts itself. Of course, I have since written a critique of that approach, which you can find in the first chapter of *Capitalism, Socialism, Ecology*: *You should never, never, try to found a political movement that intends to be emancipatory or revolutionary on a material necessity, never*. If it is a material necessity it cannot be an emancipatory movement. You can only take advantage of a necessity in order to further something that you have wanted anyway. Use it as a tool, but do not build on it, which is something that I was doing, wrongly, when I wrote the article 'Ecology and Revolution'. This was theorising the reconciliation between science and revolution. You cannot found revolution on science. So I am very self-critical of my original writings on ecology. But I very quickly changed from the first articles, which were published in 1972, stressing the need for an ecology that was based upon aspirations of self-determination and autonomy, rather than necessity.

JT: From the late 1970s onwards a new conception of power and of society characterised your work. You abandoned your work-based model of society and the central role previously attributed to the working class within processes of social change. Central to this fundamental shift in your thinking seemed to be the belief that we were entering a new historical period, generating new problems and needing new perspectives. Was there a sense of disillusionment in having to relinquish all those ideas that had constituted your work since the 1960s?

AG: No. My conviction was and still is that the labour movement should be one of the actors of the change of perspective. Much of the 'Green' critique of industrialism, economic growth and the affluent model of consumption can be found already in *Strategy for Labour*, which I wrote in 1963. This book was quite influential with the CFDT[3] which, during the 1960s and 1970s, identified with the younger and more radicalised strata of the working class – those for whom workers' control, self-determination at the workplace, self-fulfilment, the elimination of Taylorism, piece rates, oppressive hierarchies were issues of greater importance than wage rates. The CFDT were also joining forces in the 1970s with the ecologist and anti-nuclear movements, accepting to be part of a wider alliance for change. They were pointing to the fact that atomic energy is politically dangerous, impermeable to workers' control and liable to lead to a police state. Thanks to the CFDT, the labour movement became a forum for political and cultural debates on 'changing life', on sustainable growth and renewable energies, on a different distribution of power within society. They were the first to campaign for a sizeable reduction of working hours. If you read the 'Summary' at the end of *Critique of Economic Reason*, you will notice I kept considering the labour movement as an indispensable actor in the alliance for social change that we need. But I added that it could no longer claim to hegemonise this alliance. You can no longer expect society to be changed from within the work process. Factories are no longer the decisive centres of power and decision-making. Society and self-identity are being increasingly produced when people are not 'at work'.

JT: Do you become frustrated when unions still persist with quantitative, rather than qualitative, demands and do you think that this situation is changing?

AG: The only thing that prevents governments from dismantling the welfare state, deregulating, abolishing public services, reducing wages, benefits and pensions is the fear that the railways, airlines, urban transport systems, electricity, gas, the post and schools would all go on strike … In France, when the airline workers were on strike and blocked the runways, 73 per cent of French people thought that they were right, because everybody nowadays is afraid that they are going to cut your wages, fire you and give you a temporary job and reduce your pension rights, and so on. They recognise their own fear in the fear of these people who run the strikes and will approve of them striking again, whatever the nuisance.

JT: So there is an increasing legitimacy crisis?

AG: Yes.

JT: In *Critique of Economic Reason* you state that because everything has been taken away from the workers, the workers expect everything to be given to them by the state. Has this situation changed to the extent that people no longer expect to get everything from the state and, indeed, feel that it is increasingly acting in a manner which contradicts their interests, thereby fuelling this crisis of legitimacy?

AG: People fear that market competition is going to take everything away from them and that the only machine that can protect them from this is a strong state. So we have got defensively the same situation that was taken up offensively in the 1950s and the 1960s. People don't expect anything from the state anymore, they don't rely on it, but they are afraid that they can no longer rely on anything. I sympathise with this attitude; what else can you propose? You can only say that we will completely restructure the welfare state and have a welfare state that is run by the people themselves and not from above down – a different form of welfare institution that will take different forms of solidarity and social co-operation.

JT: In *Critique of Economic Reason* the nature of your focus on work became more generalised. Reading articles in *Capitalism in Crisis and Everyday Life*, in comparison, much of your analysis focused upon process workers. What are the reasons behind this change?

AG: *Critique of Economic Reason* is especially devoted to the critique of the notion of work, of labour in the economic sense. I was concerned with issues that would distinctly show the irrationality of the system.

JT: Given the irrationality of the system, but also the reluctance of many in positions of authority to acknowledge it, do you think that the system is 'digging its own grave' or, alternatively, that circumstances will continue to become more irrational and barbaric?

AG: That depends on what political use we shall make of that crisis.

JT: Is there reason for a guarded optimism over the prospect of a less work-centred society? Might measures, conceived as an emergency response to Europe's twenty million unemployed, stimulate new interests, feelings, and values which would make a further reduction in working hours more feasible?

AG: That is the trend. Almost all European governments now contemplate subsidising part-time workers so as to spread employment to more people. Those in stable full-time employment have become a minority already.

JT: Within a context in which these proposed changes are not being complemented by a transformation of power relations within work or the wider society, it seems that they do not constitute a development towards a more civilised society. Do you feel that there is a danger that an expansion of free time on these terms, and without an increasing provision of communal resources, will encourage a parallel expansion of privatistic and gratuitous, rather than autonomous, activities?

AG: Yes and no. The fact that these issues are being discussed gives legitimacy to social movements that are developing: the whole network of associations, of co-operatives, of activities of social value that need to rely on secured income, but not on wages. You can no longer rely on capital to valorise all of the labour force and all the potential for activity that is available. So you have to develop forms of activity, of work if you prefer, that are not dependent upon the valorisation of capital. Which means that you move out of the capital-based society in so far as the sphere of capital valorisation becomes less and less significant in the production of society. Society is being increasingly produced by activities that are not related to the valorisation of capital.

JT: Where is this development most evident?

AG: In France, Italy, Britain, the Netherlands, North America ... In Italy and northern France you have the development of co-operative forms of activity, of networks of self-supporting creation of wealth, that are completely outside the capitalist sphere and outside the sphere of state control. All the state is being asked to do in this respect is to help these forms of activity to find spaces within society, spaces within the neighbourhoods and cities, and provide the tools which they can use to promote auto-production of co-operative services and even of small industries.

JT: So the governments are funding these projects?

AG: No, but there will be increasing pressure to get them to support them.

JT: And you see this as potentially a step towards qualitative social change?

AG: Yes.

JT: Why do you say that? It presents the potential of establishing more reciprocal relationships, but how do we go from there to a situation in which the only power which exists is that which is functionally necessary? How is this transition to be made?

AG: It is a bit early to say. It depends on the speed with which capitalist societies disintegrate and social movements develop, but it has certainly started already with the militant support of associations that are mainly of Christian origin. They are not religious but they are, let us say, solidaristic cultures.

JT: In *Socialism and Revolution* you said that the primary reason for depoliticisation, in both capitalist and socialist societies, was the fact that as a producer and a citizen the individual is deprived of all real power over the conditions in which they work. As a consequence of this, the individual is portrayed as submitting to society, rather than consciously creating it. Within this context the tendency is to withdraw into the private sphere, as a refuge in which the individual has some control. Isn't this still the case today with regard to advanced capitalist societies? And doesn't this require that agents desiring social change intervene within the social infrastructure and provide a forum for communication?

AG: Most definitely.

JT: Have you any ideas as to how this might be achieved successfully? A related problem would appear to be that of the provision of social resources.

AG: The issue is that as long as society is being produced mainly through the mediation of commercial production and waged work, there is no other solution than to withdraw into private life. But presently it is quite obvious that the time outside of waged work is no longer being thought of, or even experienced as, a space outside of society. It is increasingly becoming a central place for the production of society. If we are no longer bound or even capable of engaging in waged work all year around and for the majority of our life, what are we going to do for the rest of our time and our life? We have to find ways of relating to each other socially, producing forms of socialisation, of sociality, that are not related to the capitalist system of production and to waged work. How? Through associations, co-operatives, places where people can meet, discuss and determine collectively what their needs are and what their activities should be. The spaces created for the development of non-waged work and self-determined forms of sociality need to receive public recognition and also, therefore, some form of funding. That is the programme of a modern socialist party.

JT: Is that the programme of the socialist party succeeding the communists in Italy?

AG: Hardly, but there is a so-called movement in that direction: the 'social centres'. It started in Naples. The unemployed people of Naples have organised centres for discussion and self-determined activity, and everyone has marvelled that such a thing should exist. The Partito Democratico della Sinistra is now supporting them. You have also got some very respectable philosophers and economists who are now theorising the movement from abstract to concrete work ... Whereas under Marxism one always moved from concrete to abstract work, as a sort of promotion of universality, now universalism moves the other way; towards self-controlled, concrete work, which is not waged because its usefulness can no longer be judged in terms of monetary values.

JT: Do you have any idea of a time-span in which your proposals, or changes of a similar nature, might take place? You say that a non-class of non-workers is coming into being, prefiguring a non-society in which social classes will be abolished along with work itself. In very general terms, what kind of period did you have in mind when you suggested this?

AG: If it doesn't happen in the next ten years it may never happen. If society first disintegrates completely I do not know how long it will take before anything else becomes possible. You may have South American conditions, like in Brazil or Peru, where all you have got is the Mafia, modern capital exploiting child labour, while 80 per cent of the people are destitute, collecting garbage and rendering menial services to the rich. You have it already in big cities in the United States of America.

JT: Do you not feel that a decade is a relatively short period of time for a social movement to develop and realise its potential?

AG: We have a generation now which has become aware of these things, or even two generations. If they do not succeed I don't know what may come afterwards.

List of Main Works by Gorz

Le Traître, Paris: Editions du Seuil, 1958. First English edition of *The Traitor* translated by Richard Howard, New York: Simon and Schuster, 1959. Second English edition, revised by Gorz, London: Verso, 1989.

La Morale de l'histoire, Paris: Editions du Seuil, 1959.

Stratégie ouvrière et néocapitalisme, Paris: Editions du Seuil, 1964. *Strategy for Labour: A Radical Proposal*, translated by Martin A. Nicolaus and Victoria Ortiz, Boston: Beacon Press, 1967.

Le Socialisme difficile, Paris: Editions du Seuil, 1967. *Socialism and Revolution*, translated by Norman Denny, London: Allen Lane, 1975.

Réforme et révolution, Paris: Editions du Seuil, 1969.

Critique de la division du travail, Paris: Editions du Seuil, 1973.

The Division of Labour: the Labour Process and Class Struggle in Modern Capitalism, (ed. and co-author), Hassocks: Harvester, 1977.

Ecologie et politique, Paris: Editions Galilée, 1975; *Ecologie et liberté*, Paris: Editions Galilée, 1977 (under the names of Gorz and Michel Bosquet). *Ecology as Politics*, translated by Patsy Vigderman and Jonathan Cloud, London: Pluto Press, 1980.

Fondements pour une morale, Paris: Editions Galilée, 1977.

Adieux au Prolétariat, Paris: Editions Galilée, 1980. *Farewell to the Working Class: An Essay on Post-Industrial Socialism*, translated by Michael Sonenscher, London: Pluto Press, 1982.

La Chemins du paradis. L'agonie du capital, Paris: Editions Galilée, 1983. *Paths to Paradise: On the Liberation from Work*, translated by Malcolm Imrie, London: Pluto Press, 1985.

Métamorphoses du Travail. Quête du sens. Critique de la raison économique, Paris: Editions Galilée, 1988. *Critique of Economic Reason*, translated by Gillian Handyside and Chris Turner, London: Verso, 1989.

Capitalisme, Socialisme, Ecologie: desorientations, orientations, Paris: Editions Gaililée, 1991. *Capitalism, Socialism, Ecology*, translated by Chris Turner, London: Verso, 1994.

As Michel Bosquet

Critique du capitalisme quotidien, Paris: Editions Galilée, 1973.
  Capitalism in Crisis and Everyday Life, translated by John Howe,
  Hassocks: Harvester, 1977.
'The "Prison Factory"', *New Left Review*, no. 73, 1972.
'The Meaning of "Job Enrichment"', in Theo, Nichols (ed.),
  Capital and Labour: A Marxist Primer, Glasgow: Fontana, 1980.

Selection of articles available in English

'Aspects of Italian Communism', in Ralph Miliband and John
  Saville (eds), *The Socialist Register*, London: Merlin, 1964.
'Work and Consumption', in Perry Anderson and Robin Blackburn
  (eds), *Towards Socialism*, Glasgow, Fontana, 1966.
'Sartre and Marx', *New Left Review*, no. 52, 1968.
'Reform or Revolution', in Ralph Miliband and John Saville (eds),
  The Socialist Register, London: Merlin, 1968.
'The Pompidou Regime', *New Left Review*, no. 37, 1966.
'Immigrant Labour', *New Left Review*, no. 61, 1970.
'Technical Intelligence and the Capitalist Division of Labour',
  Telos, no. 12, Summer 1972.
'Workers Control Is More Than Just That', in Gerry G. Hunnius,
  David G. Garson and John Case (eds), *Workers Control: A Reader
  on Labour and Social Change*, New York: Vintage, 1973.
'The Tyranny of the Factory: Today and Tomorrow', *Telos*, no.
  16, 1973.
'Jean-Paul Sartre: From Consciousness to Praxis', *Philosophy Today*,
  vol. 19, no. 4, 1975.
'Sartre and the Deaf', *Telos*, no. 33, 1977.
'On the German Non-Response to the Polish Crisis: An Interview
  with André Gorz', *Telos*, no. 51, 1982.
'What, Then, Is Freedom? Reply to Bahro', *Telos*, no. 51, 1982.
'The Limits of Self-Determination and Self-Management: An
  Interview with André Gorz', *Telos*, no. 55, 1983.
'The Reconquest of Time', *Telos*, no. 55, 1983.
'Security: Against What? For What? With What?', *Telos*, no. 58,
  1983.
'The American Model and the Future of the French Left', *Telos*,
  no. 64, 1985.
'Against Confusing Autonomous Activity with Wage Labour',
  Telos, no. 64, 1985.
'The Socialism of Tomorrow', *Telos*, no. 67, 1986.
'Reshaping the Welfare State: The Conservative Approach and Its
  Socialist Alternative', *Praxis International*, vol. 6, no. 1, 1986.

'Making Space for Everyone', *New Statesman and Society*, 25 November 1988.

'A Land of Cockayne?' (Interview by John Keane), *New Statesman and Society*, 12 May 1989.

'World of No Workers' (Interview by Ed Vulliamy), *The Weekend Guardian*, 9–10 December 1989.

'The New Agenda', *New Left Review*, no. 184, 1990.

'On the Difference Between Society and Community, and Why Basic Income Cannot by Itself Confer Membership of Either', in Philippe Van Parijs (ed.), *Arguing for a Basic Income*, London: Verso, 1992.

'Post Industrial Society', *New Times*, no. 40, 24 July 1993.

'Political Ecology: Expertocracy Versus Self-Limitation', *New Left Review*, no. 202, 1993.

References

Introduction

1. Herbert Gintis, on the back cover of André Gorz, *Ecology as Politics* (London: Pluto Press, 1987).
2. For the record, Marcuse states in his Introduction:

   One-Dimensional Man will vacillate throughout between two contradictory hypotheses : (1) that advanced industrial society is capable of containing qualitative change for the foreseeable future; (2) that forces and tendencies exist which may break this containment and explode the society. I do not think that a clear answer can be given. Both tendencies are there, side by side – and even the one in the other. (Herbert Marcuse, *One-Dimensional Man* (London: Abacus, 1972) p. 13.)
3. Tony Bennett, 'Media, "Reality", Signification', in Michael Gurevitch et al. (eds), *Culture, Society and the Media* (London: Methuen, 1982) p. 308.
4. Ibid.
5. Jürgen Habermas, 'A Philosophico-Political Profile', *New Left Review*, vol. 151 (1985) p. 85.
6. Martin Jay, *Adorno* (London: Fontana, 1984) p. 11.
7. Bob Jessop, *The Capitalist State : Marxist Theories and Methods* (Oxford: Martin Robinson, 1982) p. 144.
8. André Gorz, *The Traitor* (London: Verso, 1989) p. 286.
9. Ibid.
10. Ibid.
11. Ibid, pp. 286–7.
12. André Gorz, *Capitalism, Socialism, Ecology* (London: Verso, 1994) p. 2.
13. Jean-Paul Sartre, *Between Existentialism and Marxism* (London: Verso, 1983) p. 256.

Chapter 1: Victim and Accomplice

1. André Gorz, *Fondements pour une morale* (Paris: Editions Galilée, 1977) p. 11. The translations from this text are our own, aided by Gorz himself.

2. Ibid.
3. André Gorz, *Le Traître* (Paris: Editions du Seuil, 1958), foreword by Jean-Paul Sartre. Translated into English as *The Traitor* (London: Verso, 1989). This edition includes Sartre's foreword, 'Of Rats and Men', and an afterword entitled 'A Discussion with André Gorz on Alienation, Freedom, Utopia and Himself', the transcription of an interview conducted in West Germany in 1983. This text will subsequently be referred to by its English title.
4. 'In a very real sense, it appears that ... Gorz has returned to the "vintage" existentialism of the early Sartre and his own youth' (Arthur Hirsch, *The French Left: A History and Overview* (Montreal: Black Rose Books, 1982) p. 242). Hirsch points out that Dick Howard also noted this tendency as early as 1971. See also 'Afterword: A Discussion with André Gorz on Alienation, Freedom, Utopia and Himself', *The Traitor*; particularly pages 274–8.
5. 'It was a crazy project, originally intended to run to three volumes: the first was to be about the subject in relation to itself and the world, a relation which, of course, is always partly determined by others; the second was to be about the subject's relation to other subjects; the third about how the subject relates to society and to the collective.' ('Afterword', *The Traitor*, p. 275.)
6. Finn Bowring, 'The Life and Thought of Gorz', Lancaster University, December 1993, p. 3 (unpublished).
7. Finn Bowring, 'Gorz: Ecology, System and Lifeworld', *Capitalism, Nature, Socialism*, vol. 6, no. 4, December 1995, p. 65. Of course, while *Being and Nothingness* has frequently been thought of as a work which is concerned with ethics, it purports to be an ontology. In other words, it is a description of what *is* the case, rather than what *ought* to be. And while the text ends with a series of questions for a 'future work' which could only be answered 'on the ethical plane' (p. 638), with the adoption of a new philosophical direction, Sartre eventually abandoned his project to produce an 'existentialist ethics'.
8. Indeed, the similarities between the quotes cited in references 1 and 7 are quite striking and serve to further clarify the nature of Gorz's enquiry in *Fondements pour une morale*.
9. Gorz, *Fondements*, p. 14.
10. See in particular Maurice Merleau-Ponty, *Adventures of the Dialectic* (London: Heinemann, 1974).
11. Or *pour-soi*, to use Sartre's original terminology.
12. Gorz, 'Afterword', *The Traitor*, p. 275. He continues: 'These planes are: 1. physical existence and its immediate

environment, which is always culturally and socially determined, although usually blurred or repressed; 2. the immediate present of perceptual consciousness; 3. goal-orientated practice. These three planes ... have three corresponding types of values: the vital, the aesthetic and the ethical-practical, which can never be unified or reduced to a common denominator ... all may come together in the same person ... but not at the same moment ... The ideal is an existence in which one can move smoothly between planes without having to sacrifice or subordinate any one of them.'

13. For a comprehensive overview of these debates see Mark Poster, *Existential Marxism in Post-War France* (Princeton: Princeton University Press, 1975).

14. Jean-Paul Sartre, *Critique of Dialectical Reason*, vol. 1 (London: Verso, 1991).

15. Gorz, *Fondements*, p. 18.

16. Ibid.

17. Ibid. Here, Gorz refers to himself in the third person in a manner reflecting his alienation from the person that he was. In *The Traitor* he uses a similar technique in order to demonstrate his continuing estrangement from himself within the present.

18. Ibid.

19. While Sartre, for example, decided against publishing his autobiography, *Les Mots*, in its original and most radical form, explaining that 'there is no reason to drag a poor creature through the mud just because he writes', Gorz, by way of comparison, and in Sartre's own words, gave us the opportunity to read a truly radical book. See Laura Marcus, 'An Invitation to Life: Gorz's *The Traitor*', *New Left Review*, no. 194, July/August 1992, p. 117.

20. As Marcus has observed, it is a text which situates itself neither within the great western cultural tradition nor the French line of autobiographical writing. Ibid, p. 114.

21. Bowring, 'Life', p. 3.

22. Ibid. In this respect the method employed by Gorz has been defined by Marcus as 'an application of Sartre's "progressive-regressive" method as a means of understanding the relationship between the individual and the social world'. Within this model 'the movement of comprehension is simultaneously progressive (towards the objective result) and regressive (I go back towards the original condition)'. 'Invitation', p. 118. Interestingly Gorz reports of discussions with Sartre on this approach while awaiting feedback on his

original manuscript for *Fondements pour une morale*. (Gorz, *Fondements*, p. 18.)

23. Marcus, 'Invitation', p. 114.
24. Bowring, 'Life', p. 3.
25. Gorz, *The Traitor*, p. 162.
26. Ibid, p. 146.
27. Ibid.
28. Ibid, p. 148.
29. Ibid, p. 147.
30. Gorz, *Fondements*, p. 11.
31. Gorz, *The Traitor*, p. 42.
32. Gorz, *Fondements*, p. 12.
33. Ibid.
34. Gorz, *The Traitor*, pp. 39–40.
35. Gorz, *Fondements*, p. 12.
36. Gorz, *The Traitor*, p. 40.
37. Ibid, p. 35.
38. Gorz, *Fondements*, p. 12.
39. Ibid, p. 13.
40. Ibid, p. 15.
41. Bowring, 'Gorz', p. 65.
42. Gorz, *Fondements*, p. 15.
43. Gorz, *The Traitor*, pp. 213–14.
44. Ibid, p. 35.
45. While it is clear that Gorz was being overly self-critical here, this criticism does demonstrate a recognition of the paradox that to follow Sartre's philosophy of freedom too slavishly would be a betrayal of that philosophy and, ultimately, of his own freedom.
46. Gorz, *The Traitor*, p. 36.
47. Ibid. (Our emphasis.)
48. Jean-Paul Sartre, 'Of Rats and Men', foreword to *The Traitor*, p. 30.
49. Ibid, p. 14.
50. Bowring, 'Life', p. 2.
51. 'Gorz' is a pseudonym adopted while writing *The Traitor*, the political content of which may have jeopardised his application for French citizenship. His original name was Gerhart Horst, after Gerhart Hauptmann, the German naturalist, dramatist, novelist and poet awarded the Nobel prize for literature in 1912.
52. Gorz, *The Traitor*, p. 125.
53. Ibid, p. 251.
54. Ibid, pp. 251–2.
55. Ibid, p. 255.

56. Bowring, 'Life', p. 4.

The individual in the ordinary circumstances of living may feel more unreal than real; in a literal sense, more dead than alive; precariously differentiated from the rest of the world, so that his identity and autonomy are always in question. He may lack the experience of his own temporal continuity. He may not possess an over-riding sense of personal consistency or cohesiveness. He may feel more insubstantial than substantial, and unable to assume that the stuff he is made of is genuine, good, valuable. (R.D. Laing, *The Divided Self* (Harmondsworth: Pelican, 1965) p. 42.)

57. Gorz, *The Traitor*, pp. 127–8.
58. Bowring, 'Life', p. 3.
59. Gorz, *The Traitor*, p. 74.
60. Ibid, pp. 55–6.
61. Ibid, p. 253.
62. Bowring, 'Life', p. 4.
63. Gorz, *The Traitor*, p. 98.
64. Bowring, 'Life', p. 3.
65. That of the proportion of historical, social and individual fatality and that of freedom. See 'Afterword', *The Traitor*, pp. 272–3.
66. Ibid, p. 80.
67. It is worth noting that, as Marcus has observed, for Gorz, 'nothingness' is primarily a predicament and a pathological state to be overcome; whereas for Sartre 'it is almost a neutral term, a logical and metaphysical category as much as an existentialist dilemma'. (Marcus, 'Invitation', p. 118.)
68. Gorz, *The Traitor*, p. 43.
69. Ibid, p. 260.
70. This emphasis afforded to the subjective dimensions of alienation does not prevent Gorz from acknowledging that the existing social and economic order remains 'the final and determinate reason for man's impossibility'. However, for the early Gorz, like the early Sartre, it was not sufficient to seek a solution to all our problems through social and political action alone.
71. Gorz, *The Traitor*, p. 117. (Our emphasis.)
72. Ibid, p. 91. As Marcus notes, Gorz's analysis of the exclusion and weakness which characterised his childhood owes much to Sartre's *Anti-Semite and Jew*. However, in repeatedly referring to his half-caste status, Gorz blurs Sartre's distinction between the 'authentic' and 'inauthentic' Jew. This raises the question of what would be involved in observing Sartre's

diktat that 'Jewish authenticity consists in choosing oneself as Jew'. (Marcus, 'Invitation', p. 118.)

73. Ibid.
74. Ibid, p. 106.
75. Ibid, p. 96.
76. Ibid, p. 139.
77. Ibid, pp. 139–40.
78. Ibid, p. 134.
79. Ibid, p. 138.
80. Bowring, 'Life', p. 7.
81. Ibid, p. 6.
82. Ibid.
83. Gorz, *The Traitor*, p. 71.
84. Bowring, 'Life', p. 9.
85. Ibid, p. 10.
86. Gorz, *The Traitor*, p. 152.
87. Bowring, 'Life', p. 10.
88. Gorz, *The Traitor*, p. 152.
89. Bowring, 'Life', p. 10.
90. Gorz, *The Traitor*, pp. 155–6.
91. Ibid, p. 159.
92. See Bowring, 'Life', pp. 12–13.
93. Ibid, p. 13.
94. Gorz, *The Traitor*, p. 203.
95. Bowring, 'Life', pp. 13–17.
96. Gorz, *The Traitor*, p. 215.
97. 'The neutral ethic of total refusal': 'Neutral for the impossibility of choosing anything effectively, and total refusal for the contestation of all choices, refused by virtue of their equal contingency'; Ibid, p. 209.
98. Bowring, 'Life', p. 14.
99. Gorz, *The Traitor*, p. 216.
100. Bowring, 'Life', p. 15.
101. Gorz, *The Traitor*, p. 218.
102. Ibid, pp. 230–1.
103. Bowring, 'Life', p. 15.
104. Gorz, *The Traitor*, p. 236.
105. Ibid, p. 220.
106. See Gorz, *The Traitor*, p. 276, for more on this issue.
107. Gorz, *Fondements*, p. 23.
108. Ibid.
109. Gorz writes, for example, 'What deserves to be called "evil" is facticity insofar as it cannot be salvaged, cannot be mediated into the means of a positive human accomplishment' (*Fondements*, p. 111).
110. Gorz, *The Traitor*, p. 249.

111. Ibid, p. 264.
112. Ibid.
113. Ibid.
114. 'What he considered the most important thing that he had to do from 1958 onwards was not existential philosophy: it was a matter of renewing and providing the basis for Marxism, of showing, among other things, that the proletarian revolution, or the proletariat, were only of interest inasmuch as the working class actually embodied a moral philosophy, or a moral imperative, superior to that of the bourgeoisie, which in fact Marxism constantly affirmed in its propaganda, and constantly denied, as a product of idealism, in its theory.' (Gorz, *Fondements*, p. 19.)
115. Gorz, *The Traitor*, p. 270.
116. Ibid, p. 276.

Chapter 2: The Socialism of the Early Gorz

1. André Gorz, *The Traitor* (London: Verso, 1989) p. 265.
2. Ibid. By 'historical negativity' Gorz means 'everything tending toward an appropriation of the world by men and of the history which they produce in fact'.
3. André Gorz, *La Morale de l'histoire* (Paris: Editions du Seuil, 1959).
4. Gorz joined *Les Temps Modernes* in 1961. Under the pseudonym of Michel Bosquet, which he adopted in 1951, Gorz was one of the founders of *Le Nouvel Observateur*, a leftist weekly. A collection of his essays from this was published as *Capitalism in Crisis and Everyday Life* (Hassocks: Harvester, 1977). Gorz, in fact, is a second pseudonym. For full details see Finn Bowring, 'André Gorz: An Existential Legacy', doctoral thesis, Lancaster University (1996).
5. André Gorz, *Strategy for Labour: A Radical Proposal* (Boston: Beacon Press, 1967). First published in 1964 by Editions du Seuil, Paris. *Socialism and Revolution* (London: Allen Lane, 1975) was first published in 1967 by Editions du Seuil, Paris, as *La Socialisme Difficile*.
6. Among the most influential of these studies were: John H. Goldthorpe et al., *The Affluent Worker in the Class Structure* (Cambridge: Cambridge University Press, 1969). This was the third of a three-volume study. Serge Mallet, *The New Working Class* (Nottingham: Spokesman Books, 1975). First published by Editions du Seuil, Paris in 1963. Robert Blauner, *Alienation and Freedom: The Factory Worker and his Industry* (Chicago: University of Chicago Press, 1964).

7. Gorz, *The Traitor*, p. 279.
8. For reviews of New Left thinking in France, see Hirsch, *The French Left:* Poster, *Existential Marxism*.
9. Hirsch, *The French Left*, p. 143.
10. Ibid, p. 222.
11. Poster, *Existential Marxism*, pp. 362–3.
12. Gorz, *Strategy*, p. 3.
13. Ibid, p. 104.
14. Gorz, *Socialism*, p. 235.
15. Gorz, *Strategy*, p. x.
16. Ibid. (Our emphasis.)
17. Ibid, p. 70.
18. Gorz, *Socialism*, p. 100.
19. Gorz, *Strategy*, pp. 76–7.
20. Ibid, p. 77.
21. Ibid, p. 80.
22. Ibid.
23. Ibid, p. 90.
24. Ibid, p. 89.
25. Ibid, p. 90.
26. Ibid, p. 88.
27. Ibid, pp. 87–8.
28. Gorz, *Socialism*, pp. 226–7.
29. Gorz, *Strategy*, p. 95.
30. Gorz, *Socialism*, p. 227.
31. Ibid, p. 99.
32. Ibid.
33. Gorz, *Strategy*, p. 71.
34. Ibid, pp. vii–viii.
35. Gorz, *Socialism*, p. 105.
36. Gorz, *Strategy*, p. 5.
37. Ibid.
38. Ibid.
39. Gorz, *Socialism*, p. 188.
40. Ibid.
41. Ibid, p. 189.
42. Ibid, pp. 189–90.
43. Gorz, *Strategy*, pp. 36–7.
44. Ibid, p. 37.
45. Ibid.
46. Gorz, *Socialism*, p. 33.
47. Gorz, *Strategy*, pp. 60–1. (Our emphasis.)
48. Gorz, *Socialism*, p. 26.
49. Ibid, p. 136.
50. Ibid, p. 32.
51. Ibid, pp. 167–8.

52. Ibid, pp. 35–6.
53. Ibid, pp. 60–1.
54. Ibid, p. 61.
55. Ibid, pp. 63–4.
56. Gorz, *Strategy*, p. 107.
57. Ibid, p. 105.
58. Ibid, p. 116.
59. Gorz, *Socialism*, p. 93.
60. This was Gorz's principal argument in his contribution to André Gorz (ed.), *The Division of Labour: The Labour Process and Class Struggle in Modern Capitalism* (Hassocks: Harvester, 1976). First published in 1973 by Editions du Seuil, Paris.
61. Gorz, 'Technology, Technicians and the Class Struggle', in Gorz, *Division of Labour*, p. 174.
62. Ibid, pp. 174–5. (Our emphasis.)
63. Gorz, 'Preface', in Gorz, *Division of Labour*, p. xi.
64. Gorz, 'The tyranny of the factory: today and tomorrow', in Gorz, *Division of Labour*, p. 57.
65. Gorz, *Socialism*, p. 27.
66. Gorz, 'Technology', in Gorz, *Division of Labour*, p. 179.
67. Gorz, *Socialism*, p. 27.
68. Ibid, pp. 27–8.
69. Gorz, 'Technology', in Gorz, *Division of Labour*, p. 182.

Chapter 3: Gorzian Themes

1. Sean Sayers, 'Gorz on Work and Liberation', *Radical Philosophy*, no. 58 (Summer 1991) pp. 16–17.
2. Herbert Marcuse, *Counterrevolution and Revolt* (Boston: Beacon Press, 1972) pp. 33–4.
3. Gorz, *Capitalism*, p. 99.
4. Gorz, *Strategy*, p. 128.
5. Ibid.
6. Gorz, *Critique of Economic Reason* (London: Verso, 1989) p. 177.
7. Ibid.
8. Gorz, *Paths to Paradise: On the Liberation from Work* (London: Pluto Press, 1985) p. 118.
9. Gorz, *The Traitor*, pp. 286–7.
10. Ibid, p. 282.
11. Ibid, p. 287.
12. Ibid.
13. Ibid, p. 288.
14. Gorz, *Critique*, p. 177.
15. Ibid.

16. Gorz, *Paths*, pp. 65–6.
17. Ibid, p. 66.
18. Gorz, *Ecology,* p. 34.
19. Ibid. (Our emphasis.)
20. Ibid, p. 36. It can be noted that Gorz's essay, 'Social Self-Regulation and Regulation from Outside: Civil Society and the State', *Ecology,* pp. 34–40, predates Habermas's 'colonization of the lifeworld' thesis (Jürgen Habermas, *The Theory of Communicative Action: The Critique of Functionalist Reason*, vol. 2 (Cambridge: Polity Press, 1987)). While Gorz has engaged with Habermas's thesis, and is sympathetic towards it, he has subjected Habermas's notion of 'lifeworld' to an existential critique. See Gorz, *Critique*, pp. 173–80.
21. Ibid, p. 35.
22. Gorz, *Capitalism*, p. 22.
23. Ibid, p. 23
24. Gorz, *The Traitor*, p. 284. (Our emphasis.)
25. Ibid, p. 286.
26. Ibid, p. 282.
27. Gorz, *Farewell to the Working Class* (London: Pluto Press, 1982) p. 91.
28. Gorz, *The Traitor*, p. 291.
29. Gorz, *Paths*, p. 51.
30. Ibid.
31. Gorz, *Farewell*, p. 67.
32. Ibid, p. 71.
33. Ibid, p. 76.
34. Gorz, *Critique*, p. 36.
35. Ibid.
36. Ibid, p. 37. (Our emphasis.)
37. Gorz refers to Ivan Illich, *Medical Nemesis: The Expropriation of Health* (New York: Pantheon, 1976) in *Ecology*, p. 53, n. 23.
38. Gorz, *Paths*, pp. 57–8.
39. Gorz, *Critique*, p. 165.
40. Ibid, p. 166. (Our emphasis.)
41. Ibid.
42. Gorz, *Farewell*, pp. 80–1.
43. Ibid, p. 36.
44. Ibid, p. 67.
45. Gorz, *Paths*, p. 69.
46. Gorz, *Farewell*, p. 100.
47. Ibid, p. 101.
48. Ibid.
49. Gorz, *Critique*, p. 77.
50. Gorz, *Capitalism*, p. 47.
51. Ibid, p. 49.

52. Ibid, pp. 51–2.
53. Gorz, *Critique*, p. 165.
54. Ibid, pp. 166–7.
55. Ibid, p. 167.
56. Ibid, p. 168.
57. Ibid, pp. 158–9.
58. Ibid, pp. 140–1.
59. Ibid, pp. 139–40.
60. Gorz, *Capitalism*, p. 54.
61. For a fuller treatment of Gorzian-inspired analysis of the relation between work, needs and consumerism, see Conrad Lodziak, *Manipulating Needs: Capitalism and Culture* (London: Pluto Press, 1995).
62. Gorz, *Critique*, p. 115.
63. Herbert Marcuse, *One-Dimensional Man* (London: Abacus, 1972) p. 21.
64. Gorz, *Strategy*, pp. 33–4.
65. Gorz, *Critique*, pp. 115–16.
66. See, for example, Witold Rybczynski, *Waiting for the Weekend* (New York: Viking, 1991).
67. Gorz, *Ecology*, p. 57.
68. Gorz, *Strategy*, p. 88.
69. Gorz, *Ecology*, p. 30.
70. Ibid, p. 31. Here Gorz refers to Ivan Illich, *Tools for Conviviality* (New York: Harper and Row, 1973).
71. Gorz, *Paths*, p. 16.
72. Ibid.
73. Gorz again refers to Illich, *Tools*.
74. Gorz, *Ecology*, p. 60.
75. Ibid, p. 89.
76. Ibid, p. 88.
77. Gorz, *Critique*, p. 46.
78. Gorz, *Ecology*, p. 38.
79. Gorz, *Critique*, pp. 143–4.
80. Gorz, *Farewell*, especially pp. 66–74.
81. Gorz, *Capitalism*, p. 60.
82. Gorz, *Farewell*, p. 126.
83. Ibid, p. 28.
84. Gorz, *Capitalism*, pp. 44–52.
85. For example, Robert Bocock, *Consumption* (London: Routledge, 1993).
86. See, for example, Lodziak, *Manipulating Needs*; Josephine Logan 'Privatism, Needs and Social Power: An Exploration of Human Motivation in Contemporary Society', doctoral thesis, University of Nottingham (1993); and Kate Soper,

Troubled Pleasures: Writings on Politics, Gender and Hedonism (London: Verso, 1990).

87. Gorz, *Critique*, p. 100.
88. Ibid. Note how this argument tends to be ignored in the writings of those who exaggerate the social and existential significance of consumerism. See, for example, Mike Featherstone, *Consumer Culture and Postmodernism* (London: Sage, 1991).
89. Gorz, *Capitalism*, pp. 33–4.
90. Donella H. Meadows et al., *The Limits to Growth* (New York: Universe Books, 1972).
91. Especially Illich, *Tools*.
92. Gorz, *Ecology*, p. 26.
93. Gorz, *Farewell*, p. 122.
94. Gorz, *Capitalism*, p. 94.
95. Ibid, p. 95.
96. Ibid, p. 30.
97. Gorz, *Critique*, p. 122.
98. Gorz, *Farewell*, p. 72.
99. Gorz, *Paths*, p. 39.
100. Gorz, *Capitalism*, p. 25.
101. Jürgen Habermas, *The Theory of Communicative Action*, vol. 1 (Cambridge: Polity Press, 1991).
102. Gorz, *Capitalism*, p. 30.
103. Ibid, pp. 30–1.
104. Gorz, *Critique*, p. 42.
105. Ibid, pp. 42–3.
106. Ibid, p. 42.
107. Gorz, *Capitalism*, p. 40.
108. Gorz, *Critique*, p. 42.
109. Ibid, p. 131.
110. Ibid.
111. Gorz, *Capitalism*, p. 40.
112. Ibid, pp. 40–1.
113. Gorz, *Critique*, p. 188.
114. Gorz, *Capitalism*, p. 8.
115. Ibid, p. 84. (Our emphasis.)
116. Ibid.
117. Gorz, *Critique*, p. 185.
118. Gorz, *Farewell*, p. 134.
119. Gorz, *Capitalism*, p. 44.
120. Ibid, p. 104.
121. Gorz, *Paths*, p. 105.
122. Ibid, pp. 101–10. Also *Critique*, pp. 219–42, and *Capitalism*, pp. 102–17.
123. Gorz, *Critique*, p. 190.

124. Ibid, p. 191
125. Ibid, p. 192.
126. Ibid, p. 193.
127. Ibid, pp. 193–4.
128. Ibid, p. 194.
129. Ibid, p. 195.
130. Ibid, pp. 199–202 and *Capitalism*, pp. 102–17.
131. Gorz, *Capitalism*, p. 105. Examples for the four options are taken from pp. 104–6.
132. Ibid.
133. Ibid, p. 107.
134. Ibid.
135. Ibid, pp. 108–12 and *Critique*, pp. 199–202, 240–2.
136. Gorz, *Paths*, p. 40.
137. Gorz, *Critique*, p. 205.
138. Ibid, p. 207.
139. Ibid, p. 211.
140. Gorz, *Capitalism*, p. 114.
141. Gorz, *Farewell*, p. 143.
142. Gorz, *Paths*, pp. 103–4.
143. Gorz, *Farewell*, pp. 86–7.
144. Gorz, *Paths*, p. 3.
145. Gorz, *Capitalism*, pp. 97–8.

Chapter 4: Gorz and His Critics

1. As early as 1969 John Goldthorpe et al. used Gorz and Marcuse interchangeably to sum up their own understanding of the 'affluent worker'. See Goldthorpe et al., *The Affluent Worker*, pp. 179–81. More recently Gorz has been described as 'an ecological Marcuse'. See J.G. Merquiror, *Western Marxism* (London: Paladin, 1986), p. 198. Anthony Giddens, too, has referred to 'many places in his work where what Gorz has to say carries more than an echo of Marcuse'. See Anthony Giddens, *Social Theory and Modern Sociology* (Cambridge: Polity Press, 1987) p. 281.
2. Gorz has been described as a Marxist and post-Marxist, Stalinist and anti-Stalinist, anarchist and existentialist. Gorz's existentialism is automatically received in some quarters as reason enough to dismiss him out of hand. Under the destructive practices of academic reductionism the complex diversity of existentialism is transformed into little more than a manifestation of the ideology of bourgeois individualism. For Dick Howard, Gorz's 'diagnosis of the end of capitalism's liberating potential leaves only existential

ontological freedom as the foundation of a future politics'. See Dick Howard, *The Marxian Legacy*, 2nd edition (London: Macmillan, 1988) p. 389, n. 70. Similarly Richard Hyman has it that 'Gorz oscillates between a highly deterministic model of the "juggernaut of capital", and (no doubt reflecting his existential background) a tendency to voluntarism and idealism'. See Richard Hyman, 'André Gorz and His Disappearing Proletariat', in Ralph Miliband and John Saville (eds), *The Socialist Register* 1983 (London: The Merlin Press, 1983) p. 292. For Adrian Atkinson, Gorz's existentialism is

> a restatement of liberal individualism rather than any development of Marxism ... Gorz's concept of an irreducible dualism ... is not Marxist at all but is a very clear reinterpretation of the French philosophical tradition from Descartes to Sartre; that life involves a struggle between an irreducible human essence and the dead machinery of the world around us. (Adrian Atkinson, *Principles of Political Ecology* (London: Belhaven, 1991) p. 33.)

Academic ignorance has caricatured existentialism not only as an ideology of bourgeois individualism, but also as a philosophy of despair, one which promotes the view that life is absurd. Ellen Meiskins Wood thus refers to 'Gorz's utopia' as 'a vision ultimately grounded in despair'. See Ellen Meiskins Wood, 'Marxism Without Class Struggle?', in Miliband and Saville, *Socialist Register 1983*, p. 244. Boris Frankel *The Post-Industrial Utopians* (Cambridge: Polity Press, 1987) asks 'If the norms and laws of a post-industrial socialist society do not correspond to the individual's needs, is Gorz merely succumbing to the old existentialist dictum that life is absurd?' (p. 159). Frankel does not know what to make of Gorz. On the one hand Gorz is an existentialist, but on the other his work 'still indicates the lasting influence of [his] Marxist heritage' (pp. 24–5). Yet Gorz has 'little understanding of political economy' (p. 94). Even though, 'in actual fact, Gorz still largely works within the Marxist framework', (p. 213) 'Gorz puts forward a rebellious anarchistic view of family relations' (p. 158). To add to this, Geoff Hodgson claims that Gorz has moved from a 'quasi-Stalinist position of the 1950s' to 'his quasi-anarchist position of today'. See Geoff Hodgson, *The Democratic Economy* (Harmondsworth: Penguin, 1984) pp. 190–1. However, for David Byrne there is no way that Gorz can be an anarchist since 'Gorz denies subjective autonomy to the working class'. See David Byrne, 'A Rejection of André Gorz's "Farewell to the Working Class"', *Capital and Class*, vol. 24. (Winter 1984–5) p. 77. And what are we to make of the absurd claim that Gorz's work has been heavily influenced by Foucault? See Johannes Berger and Norbert Kostede, 'Review of "Farewell to the Working Class"', *Telos*, vol. 51 (Spring 1982) p. 232.

3. Finn Bowring, 'Misreading Gorz,' *New Left Review*, vol. 217 (May/June 1996) p. 102. A longer version of this paper appears in Finn Bowring, 'André Gorz'. Bowring's study is the most comprehensive study of Gorz conducted. It is brilliant.

4. Chris Whitbread, 'Gorz, Nove, Hodgson: The Economics of Socialism', *Capital and Class*, vol. 26 (Summer 1985) p. 129.

5. The autonomy/heteronomy distinction is referred to in *Ecology as Politics*, p. 53, n. 23, and it does come from Illich. See Illich, *Medical Nemesis: The Expropriation of Health* (New York: Pantheon, 1976).

6. Michael Haralambos, *Sociology: Themes and Perspectives* (Slough: University Tutorial Press, 1980) p. 236.

7. Ibid, p. 357. Further, Marcuse explicitly rejects this view. See Marcuse, *One-Dimensional Man*, p. 21.

8. Chris Rojek, *Capitalism and Leisure Theory* (London: Tavistock, 1985) p. 138. Among Rojek's errors is that of attributing to Gorz the assumption that 'the wealth liberated by the ending of the class system will be devoted to improving the system of social services' (p. 138). He claims that one of the 'problems in his analysis relating to the question of the transition to socialism' is that 'Gorz portrays the transition to post-industrial socialism as an automatic process' (p. 139). One wonders what Rojek thinks the politics of time is about. And, just like the Frankfurt School, apparently, Gorz 'displays the brand-mark of functionalist reasoning'! (p. 121).

9. Murray Bookchin, *Toward an Ecological Society* (Montreal: Black Rose Books, 1980) p. 300.

10. Ibid, p. 16.

11. Ibid, p. 17.

12. Ibid.

13. Ibid, p. 18.

14. Ibid, p. 292.

15. Sean Sayers, 'Gorz on Work and Liberation', *Radical Philosophy*, no. 58 (Summer 1991) p. 18.

16. Karl Marx, 'The Holy Family', in *Collected Works*, vol. 4 (London: Lawrence and Wishart, 1975) p. 37. This quotation appears in a footnote in *Farewell*, p. 16.

17. Gorz, *Farewell*, p. 16.

18. Hyman, 'André Gorz', p. 283.

19. Gorz, *Farewell* , p. 19. (Our emphasis.)

20. Ibid, pp. 19–20. (Our emphasis.)

21. Hyman, 'André Gorz', p. 283.

22. Ibid. (Our emphasis.) Here Hyman is quoting Hal Draper, *Karl Marx's Theory of Revolution*, vol. 1 (New York: Monthly Review Press, 1977) pp. 136–7.

23. Ibid.

24. Ibid. (Our emphasis.)

25. Gorz, *Farewell*, p. 21.

26. Ibid.

27. Hyman, 'André Gorz', p. 283.

28. Ibid, pp. 283–4.

29. Ibid, p. 284. Here, Hyman quotes Shlomo Avineri, *The Social and Political Thought of Karl Marx* (London: Cambridge University Press, 1968) p. 144.

30. Ibid.

31. Gorz, *Farewell*, p. 64.

32. Ibid. Also, Gorz, *Strategy*, especially pp. 3–34.

33. Hyman mentions five sources: 1) 'The search for a "universal class" ... and the discovery of the proletariat as a class whose "radical chains" entailed that its particular emancipation could be achieved only through *general* social emancipation.' 2) 'The anthropological conception of purposeful social labour as the defining characteristic of humanity ... the proletariat's function was the embodiment of this human creativity.' 3) 'The connection with the "philosophy of practice"' in which 'the labour process could be viewed as the elemental form of human praxis and proletarian revolution its crowning manifestation'. 4) 'The labour theory of value: if labour was the foundation of social productivity, it seemed to follow that the working class was pivotal for social transformation.' 5) The immiseration thesis: 'workers would surely be driven to revolt, and would continue to revolt until they had eliminated the underlying causes of their misery'. (Hyman, 'André Gorz', p. 284.)

34. Ibid.

35. Ibid, pp. 284–5.

36. Ibid, p. 286.

37. Ibid, p. 285.

38. Ibid.

39. Ibid. The passage in question comes from Karl Marx, *Capital*, vol. 1 (Harmondsworth: Penguin, 1976) pp. 548–9.
40. Ibid.
41. Ibid, p. 286.
42. Gorz, *Strategy*, p. 286. The passage which Gorz quotes is from Karl Marx, *Grundrisse der Kritik der Politischen Oekonomie* (Berlin: Dietz, 1953) pp. 592–4, 596.
43. Marx, *Grundrisse*, p. 596.
44. Gorz, *Farewell* , pp. 81–2.
45. Marx, *Grundrisse*, p. 706.
46. Marx, *Capital*, vol. 3 (London: Lawrence and Wishart, 1959) p. 820. Gorz quotes from the above in *Farewell*.
47. Frankel, *Post-Industrial*, p. 212.
48. Gorz, *Farewell*, p. 73.
49. Ibid, p. 81.
50. Ibid. (Our emphasis.)
51. Ibid.
52. Gorz, *Paths*, p. 35.
53. Hyman, 'André Gorz', p. 287. The same criticism is made by Barry Smart in *Modern Conditions, Postmodern Controversies* (London: Routledge, 1992) p. 93.
54. Paul Ransome, *Job Security and Social Stability: The Impact of Mass Unemployment on Expectations of Work* (Aldershot: Avebury, 1995) p. 210.
55. Bowring notes that Gorz stopped using this term when it was 'adopted by a French technocrat advocating a dual economy', Bowring, 'André Gorz', p. 306.
56. Marx, *Capital*, vol. 3, p. 820.
57. Gorz, *Farewell*, p. 109. See also Gorz's critique of communalism, pp. 107–12.
58. Ibid, p. 111.
59. Sayers, 'Gorz on Work', p. 16. See also Berger and Kostede who write that Gorz presents 'an image of the factory as a hell of self-alienation ... '. In Berger and Kostede, 'Review of Farewell to the Working Class''', p. 232.
60. Sean Sayers, 'The Need to Work', in R.E. Pahl (ed.), *On Work* (Oxford: Blackwell, 1988) p. 730.
61. Hodgson, *The Democratic Economy*, p. 190 (our emphasis). Similarly Berger and Kostede argue that Gorz's model 'cannot be stabilized unless elements of autonomy and free activity are introduced into the realm of necessity' ('Review of "Farewell"' p. 232).
62. See Gorz, *Farewell*, pp. 2, 9, 86–7 and 98. See also André Gorz, *Critique*, pp. 78, 79, 93, 98, 169 and 171.
63. Giddens, *Social Theory*, p. 280.
64. Ibid, p. 295.

65. Ibid.
66. Gorz, *Ecology*, pp. 34–40.
67. Giddens, *Social Theory*, p. 285.
68. This might be unfair to Giddens. But given that he offers no compelling reasons for his assertion, he is vulnerable to the criticism that we have made. More recently, Giddens has put his weight behind already existing 'democratizing tendencies' within society. However, their connection to major social transformations is handled in a somewhat abstract way. See Anthony Giddens, *Beyond Left and Right: The Future of Radical Politics* (Cambridge: Polity Press, 1994) especially pp. 104–33.
69. Frankel, *Post-Industrial*, p. 19. Here, Frankel states: 'It is important to make clear that this book is not essentially an exposition of post-industrial theory ... there is no attempt to cover thoroughly the entire works of any specific thinker.'
70. Frankel, *Post-Industrial*, p. 60.
71. Ibid, p. 166.
72. Ibid, p. 89.
73. Gorz, *Critique*, especially pp. 135–71.
74. Sayers 'Gorz on Work'.
75. Gorz, *Critique*, p. 132.
76. Ibid, p. 237.
77. Ibid, p. 169.
78. Ibid.
79. Sayers, 'Gorz on Work', p. 18.
80. Gorz, *Critique*, pp. 146–50.
81. Richard Hyman, 'Review of André Gorz's "Critique of Economic Reason"', *Sociology*, vol. 24, no. 3 (August 1990) pp. 531–2.
82. Frankel, *Post-Industrial*, p. 93.
83. Ivan Illich, *Gender* (London: Marion Boyars, 1983) p. 65 (our emphasis).
84. Ibid. (Our emphasis.) Illich here develops the argument of Claudia von Werlhof, *Las Mujeres y la Perifia* (Bielefeld: University of Bielefeld, 1981).
85. Ibid.
86. Sayers, 'Gorz on Work', p. 18.
87. Frankel, *Post-Industrial*, p. 91.
88. Gorz, *Critique*, p. 164 (our emphasis).
89. Ibid.
90. Gorz, *Farewell*, p. 84.
91. Gorz, *Critique*, pp. 142–64.
92. Bowring, 'Misreading Gorz', University of Lancaster, unpublished (January 1995), p. 46.
93. Gorz, *Critique*, pp. 151–2.

94. Gorz, *Capitalism*, p. 63.
95. Gorz, *Socialism*, p. 219. This is taken from a lecture delivered by Gorz in 1966.
96. Ibid, p. 218.
97. Gorz, *Paths*, p. 31.
98. Gorz, *Capitalism*, p. 50. Also in *Critique*, p. 205.
99. Smart, *Modern Conditions*, p. 96.
100. Frankel, *Post-Industrial*, p. 138. Quoted in Smart, *Modern Conditions*, p. 96.
101. Smart, *Modern Conditions*, p. 96.
102. John Keane and John Owens, *After Full Employment* (London: Hutchinson, 1986) p. 169. Quoted in Smart, *Modern Conditions*, pp. 92–3.
103. Smart, *Modern Conditions*, p. 92 (our emphasis). Hyman, in 'André Gorz', makes a similar criticism. Given that Hyman is reviewing *Farewell*, his criticism does reveal an absence in *Farewell*, an absence which is made good in *Paths*. Hyman notes that: 'In discussing the integration of different systems of production, and the relationship between state and civil society, Gorz appears to assume a specifically national context. Despite the attention in many of his previous writings to issues of internationalism, this dimension is absent here', p. 292.
104. Gorz, *Paths*, pp. 101–10.
105. Gorz, *Critique*, p. 188.
106. Ibid, p. 189.
107. Giddens, *Social Theory*, p. 296.
108. Ransome, *Job Security*.
109. Ibid, p. 64.
110. Ibid, p. 124.
111. Ibid, p. 206.
112. Paul Ransome, *The Work Paradigm: A Theoretical Investigation of Concepts of Work* (Aldershot: Avebury, 1996) p. 149.
113. Ransome, *Job Security*, p. 63.
114. Bowring, 'André Gorz', p. 213.
115. Ibid, p. 190. Bowring draws on Will Hutton's calculations (*Guardian*, 3 April 1995).
116. Will Hutton, *The State We're In* (London: Jonathan Cape, 1995) pp. 105–10.
117. Smart, *Modern Conditions*, p. 94.
118. Bowring in 'André Gorz', p. 358, cites an OECD report, *Labour Supply, Growth Constraints and Work Sharing* (Paris, 1982) in which empirical evidence indicated that 'a majority of full-time employees would prefer to work less *even if they earned less*'. This report is also cited in Keane and Owens,

After Full Employment, p. 174. Strangely Smart does draw on Keane and Owens when it suits him.

Bowring also cites 'a rare American study in which two thirds of the respondents expressed a desire to trade *future* increases in earning power for increased free time'. The study is F. Best, *Flexible Life Scheduling: Breaking the Education–Work–Retirement Lockstep* (New York: Praeger, 1980), which is also cited in Paul Blyton, *Changes in Working Time: An International Perspective* (Sydney: Croom Helm, 1985) pp. 40–3. Bowring's discussion of research in this area is instructive. We quote him at length:

> The assumption that a significant number of people prefer increased consumption instead of reduced working hours derives from the results of studies which, due to the choices offered to respondents, typically underestimate the desire for more free time. This distortion of people's preferences is the result of three factors. The first is that the choice of a more fruitful, active and better resourced use of free time is not included in the choice of a reduced working week, which is concerned only with the quantity of free time and not the quality of its use.

Bowring's second point has radical implications for studies conducted within the framework of an ideology of individualism. Thus Bowring notes that 'the hypothetical choice of more "flexible" working hours is presented to the respondent as an individual choice taken in isolation from the choices of others'. Bowring goes on to make the point that: 'We have seen that the value and consequence of individual choices cannot be established without taking into account the choices of others.' He continues:

> In other words, it is hardly surprising that individuals feel reluctant to reduce their working hours when the rest of society continues to expand its consumer capacity, when the social infrastructure continues to be geared towards maximising the flow of commodities rather than satisfying felt needs, and when professionals, manufacturers, technologies and institutions continue to manipulate and colonise our preferences, conduct and time. If the choice to work less is the choice to be marginalised from a society still dedicated to the cult of consumption, many people will choose to keep their place in the status quo.

The third factor, and the most important one for Bowring, 'is that almost all the studies conducted on people's attitudes to work and free time, because they offer choices on a purely individual basis and exclude macro-economic initiatives, present the choice to work less as the option of trading a proportion of one's income for more leisure'. (Bowring, 'André Gorz', pp. 357–8.)

119. Gorz, *Farewell*, p. 13.
120. Hyman, 'André Gorz', p. 292.
121. Smart, *Modern Conditions*, p. 94.
122. See for example, Zygmunt Bauman, *Intimations of Postmodernity* (London: Routledge, 1992), and Stuart Hall and Martin Jacques (eds), *New Times: The Changing Face of Politics in the 1990s* (London: Sage, 1991) p. 14.
123. Featherstone, *Consumer Culture*, p. 14.
124. Ibid, p. 13.
125. See for example, Robert E. Lane, 'Markets and the Satisfaction of Human Wants', *Journal of Economic Issues*, vol. xii, no. 4 (December 1978). Lane cites a wide range of studies in Robert E. Lane, *The Market Experience* (London: Cambridge University Press, 1991). Several studies are also cited in Richard Douthwaite, *The Growth Illusion* (Bideford: Green Books, 1992). See also H. Sahin and J.P. Robinson, 'Beyond the Realm of Necessity: Television and the Colonization of Leisure', in *Media, Culture and Society*, vol. 3 (1980) pp. 85–95.
126. Featherstone, *Consumer*, p. 13.
127. See Lodziak, *Manipulating Needs*, especially pp. 49–51.
128. See Lodziak, *The Power of Television: A Critical Appraisal* (London: Frances Pinter, 1986) especially pp. 142–55.
129. Hyman, 'André Gorz', p. 290.
130. Marcuse, *Counterrevolution*, p. 35.
131. Jürgen Habermas, *The Past as Future* (Cambridge: Polity Press, 1994) p. 158.
132. Claus Offe, *Contradictions of the Welfare State*, edited by John Keane (London: Hutchinson, 1984) p. 283.
133. R.W. Connell, *Which Way Is Up?: Essays on Sex, Class and Culture* (London: Allen and Unwin, 1983) p. 169.
134. Ibid, p. 115.
135. Paul Thompson, *The Nature of Work: An Introduction to Debates on the Labour Process*, 2nd edition (London: Macmillan, 1989) p. 276. Cited in Finn Bowring, 'André Gorz: Ecology, System and Lifeworld', *Capitalism, Nature, Socialism*, vol. 6, no. 4 (December 1995) p. 66.
136. For example, Paul Ransome, *Work Paradigm*, pp. 175–97.
137. For example, James Robertson, *Future Work: Jobs, Self-employment and Leisure after the Industrial Age* (Aldershot: Gower, 1985).

138. For example, Alec Nove, *The Economics of Feasible Socialism* (London: Allen and Unwin, 1983).
139. For example, Andrew Dobson, *Green Political Thought: An Introduction* (London: Unwin Hyman, 1990). Dobson defends Gorz against criticisms from Frankel (pp. 164–8). Bowring, in 'André Gorz: Ecology, System and Lifeworld', defends Gorz against Bookchin's criticisms (pp. 74–5).
140. Bowring, 'Misreading Gorz', p. 102.
141. Ibid, p. 122. Bowring is referring to 'The Time Squeeze', *Demos Quarterly*, no. 5, 1995.
142. Ibid.

A Dialogue with Gorz

1. This is a transcription of a meeting between André Gorz and Jeremy Tatman at Gorz's Burgundy home on 24 November 1993. It has been reproduced with Gorz's kind permission and help.
2. Adrian Little, 'Existentialism and Communism in Post-war France: The Political Theory of André Gorz', *Reflections*, 89, The Nottingham Trent University, 1992.
3. Confédération Française Démocratique du Travail.

Index

Illich, Ivan 63, 73, 78, 93, 106–7,
109, 144, 145, 146, 149, 152
imperialism 39, 109–10
internationalism 84, 86, 110–11

Jacques, Martin 155
Jay, Martin 5, 135
Jones, Barry 104
justice and the politics of time 86

Keane, John 110, 153–4, 155
Kostede, Norbert 104, 149, 151

labour
division of 51–4, 61, 65, 102
domestic 65, 69–70, 106–8
international division of 106–7,
109, 110
movement 37–8, 46–54, 126–7
process 52–4
time 55–6, 66–7, 71–2, 77–8,
84–92, 118–19, 124, 154–5
Laing, R. D. 20, 138–9
Lane, Robert E. 155
Lefebvre, Henri 113–14
left politics 9
New Left 37–8
Old Left 37–8, 43–6, 48, 52–3
lifeworld 37–8, 43–6, 48, 52–3
Little, Adrian 124, 156
Lodziak, Conrad 145, 155
Logan, Josephine 145

Mallet, Serge 141
Marcuse, Herbert 1, 2, 55–6, 71,
93–4, 115, 135, 143, 147,
149, 155
Marcus, Laura 137, 139
Marx, Karl 6, 8, 34, 43, 61, 63,
96–100, 118, 124, 130, 141
mass media 93
May 1968 9, 38, 51–4, 125
Meadows, Donnella 146
Merleau-Ponty, Maurice 32, 136
Merquior, J. G. 147
micro-electronic technology 9, 47,
54, 77, 85, 111–12
Miliband, Ralph 148
modernisation of poverty 73
La morale de l'histoire 36, 115,
133, 141

needs
basic 39–43, 45
and capitalism 38–43
and critique of capitalism 41–2,
48
collective 41–2
and consumerism 70–6
and deskilled work 74
existential 38–40, 51, 65, 114
manipulation of 38–43
and production 71
and realm of necessity 63–4
self-limitation of 92
and socialism 45
for time 90–1
neo-proletariat 100–1
Le Nouvel Observateur 36
Nove, Alec 149, 156

Offe, Claus 115, 155
ontological insecurity 20
Owens, John 110, 153–4

Pahl, R. E. 151
Paths to Paradise 55–92, 104,
109–10, 122, 143, 144, 145,
146, 147, 151, 153
planned obsolescence 40, 75
political correctness 106, 108
political ecology 9, 76–80, 125
political parties 44
revolutionary 44–5, 49–51
vanguard 44, 51
political strategy 46–51, 84–92,
112–14
politics of time 55–6, 84–92,
118–19, 124, 154–5
Poster, Mark 38, 137, 141–2
poststructuralism 2–3
poverty 73
powerlessness 42–3
private sphere 62–4, 68
privatism 129
production 66, 74–6
and need 71
professional elites 67, 87
psychoanalysis 12, 22–3, 32,
118
psychology 8

quality of life 122